Quiet Water

Canoe Guide

Pennsylvania

Also available from Appalachian Mountain Club Books

AMC Quiet Water Canoe Guides
Massachusetts/Connecticut/Rhode Island
New Hampshire/Vermont
Alex Wilson

AMC River Guides
Maine
Massachusetts/Connecticut/Rhode Island
New Hampshire/Vermont

AMC Trail Guides
Guide to Mount Desert Island and Acadia National Park, 5th edition
Guide to Mount Washington and the Presidential Range, 5th edition
Hiking the Mountain State (West Virginia)
Maine Mountain Guide, 7th edition
Massachusetts/Rhode Island Trail Guide
North Carolina Hiking Trails, 2nd edition
White Mountain Guide, 25th edition

River Rescue
2nd edition
Les Bechdel and Slim Ray

White Water Handbook
3d Edition
Bruce Lessels

APPALACHIAN MOUNTAIN CLUB

Quiet Water

Canoe Guide

Pennsylvania

BEST PADDLING LAKES AND PONDS
FOR ALL AGES

Scott and Linda Shalaway

APPALACHIAN MOUNTAIN CLUB BOOKS
BOSTON, MASSACHUSETTS

**Due to changes in conditions, use of the
information in this book
is at the sole risk of the user.**

Contents

To our mothers
Valeria Shalaway and Pearl Fulmer,

and our daughters,
Nora and Emma.

Acknowledgments

Putting together this book was much more than an exercise in writing. It was an adventure. During the spring and summer of 1993 we traveled more than 5,000 miles across Pennsylvania as we visited and evaluated the lakes included in this book (and many others that were not included). In order to devote this much time to a single project, we relied on many people.

Our mothers, Valeria Shalaway and Pearl Fulmer, eagerly and lovingly cared for our daughters during a particularly hectic three-week stretch. Without that help, we could not have met our deadline.

Susan Lazarus, Andi Coyle, and Carolyn Neary made our summer much more pleasant and organized by offering us a lot of information about Pennsylvania and giving us the names of important contacts.

Rudy Miller's stunning pencil drawings add life and excitement to the text, and Hal Korber's cover photo still takes our breath away.

Many thanks to Kristin Gilmore, who spent hours in the darkroom printing the photographs that illustrate this book.

Gordon Hardy, editor of AMC Books, offered patience, advice, and encouragement when it was needed most.

Employees of Pennsylvania State Parks, the Game Commission, and the Fish Commission gave freely of their time and information.

And our daughters, Nora and Emma, gave us insight into their view of the quiet water experience, understood when we had to be away more than any of us liked, and gave us time to write during that frantic final stage.

To all these folks we say, "Thank you!"

How to Use This Book

We've tried to make this book as easy to use as possible. At the beginning of the book you will find an outline locator map of the state showing all the lakes described in the book. This will give you a feel for the overall distribution of the lakes across the state.

For organizational purposes, we've broken the state into six regions, the same ones used by the Pennsylvania Game Commission and the Pennsylvania Fish and Boat Commission: Northeast, Southeast, South-Central, Southwest, Northwest, and North-Central. These regions correspond to the six major sections of the book. Each section begins with its own outline map, which includes counties, major highways, and, of course, the lakes.

The accounts of each lake include a description of the area, detailed instructions explaining how to get there, an anecdote or two about something we saw or heard, and, in some cases, a brief list of significant nearby attractions.

The instructions for finding each location are designed to be used with a state highway map, available gratis at welcome centers or any Pennsylvania Turnpike rest area. Never travel without one. We also found the latest edition of the *Pennsylvania Atlas & Gazetteer* (published by the DeLorme Mapping Co., Freeport, Maine) to be invaluable. The *Gazetteer* was particularly helpful when searching for some of the more remotely located Fish Commission lakes.

Finally, scattered throughout the book you will find a series of natural history essays (written by Scott) intended to enhance your understanding of the creatures you are sure to see while paddling Pennsylvania. We suggest you read these essays before tackling the rest of the book and before you visit any lakes. They preview the natural history of the lakes described in the book and should make any canoe outing more enjoyable. The drawings by Oklahoma artist Rudy Miller were commissioned to complement the essays and the many anecdotes found in the individual lake accounts.

Introduction

Until we set out to write this book, we never really thought about "quiet water." We had paddled in whitewater rivers, smaller streams, and lakes of all sizes, but to us, it all fell under the heading of "canoeing." Now that we've become quiet water specialists, we appreciate its special appeal.

Quiet water canoeing is easy. Anyone can paddle a canoe on a small, quiet lake. It's a great family activity. Not only can children participate, grandparents and other seniors will find paddling an enjoyable outdoor experience. In fact, the most strenuous part of quiet water canoeing is putting the canoe in and out of the water.

What Is Quiet Water?

Quiet water simply refers to any body of water without a current. Rivers and streams have currents, whereas ponds, lakes, and reservoirs do not. Canoeing quiet waters does not require the same concentration as canoeing whitewater and strong currents, so there is time for serious wildlife watching. And that, we believe, is the major value of quiet water canoeing—the real reason for seeking out the state's most interesting lakes and reservoirs. The canoe is perhaps the best vehicle for close encounters with wildlife. Animals you couldn't get close to on land—beavers, otters, ducks, deer, muskrats, green-backed herons—will easily tolerate the presence of the careful quiet water canoeist.

We further define quiet waters as those undisturbed by the roar and wake of high-speed motorboats. Quiet waters should ring with the sounds of silence—and geese honking, ducks quacking, bass leaping, lily pads rustling in the breeze, herons squawking, and kingfishers chattering overhead. Thus, we intentionally chose lakes where motorboat use is restricted or prohibited. Most of the lakes administered by the Pennsylvania Fish Commission and the state's Bureau of State Parks fall into this category, so a large percentage of the lakes we recommend are state park or Fish Commission lakes.

Even where motorboats are prohibited, the quiet water canoe experience can suffer from too many people or too much road noise. So we further narrowed our selection to lakes more isolated and less crowded. Also, we purposely included many lakes with marshy or swampy areas—areas particularly attractive to wildlife.

Finally, we wanted to include lakes that could be enjoyed by almost everyone—families with young children, retired couples, and others who don't want to portage canoes for any distance. Unlike many states, most of Pennsylvania's quiet water is readily accessible. Canoeists will find graded or paved roads, toilets, launches, and parking areas.

Canoeing on quiet water is quite different from whitewater or even slow water. Whitewater requires skill, experience, concentration, and promises a fast, thrilling ride. Quiet water, on the other hand, is slow and reflective. Whitewater is macho; quiet water is cerebral. The whole point of quiet water canoeing is to become part of the environment, not just a passerby.

We like to describe quiet water canoeing as a nature walk on water. As you glide almost silently through a marsh or swamp or along a lake's edge, you will see things you just can't see from a trail on land. It's as if animals accept you as a benign part of the environment. In the course of our explorations we've had close encounters with bald eagles, ospreys, a river otter, countless turtles, marsh wrens, beavers, and many more animals that we would have missed entirely had we been on dry land. A canoe on quiet water opens up a whole new world to curious naturalists.

How We Selected the Lakes in This Book

More than 3,000 lakes and reservoirs grace the mountains, valleys, and rolling farm fields of Pennsylvania. Canoeists here can choose quiet waters of any size in practically any situation—from urban settings to the picturesque farmlands of the state's southeast and south-central sections; from the isolated mountains in the northeast and north-central counties to the southwestern Laurel Highlands; from the northwest glacial moraines to the great Lake Erie itself. This book features almost seventy lakes chosen from among this wide variety of locations. They are the "best" according to the criteria we established for a high-quality quiet water experience.

Originally we planned to feature one lake from each of the state's sixty-seven counties, but we quickly discovered that quality quiet water is not evenly distributed around the state. Most of it is in the northeast and the northwest. That's why you'll find a disproportionate number of lakes from these two regions. Eventually we decided to include the best lakes we could find, regardless of where they occurred. That's why some counties are not represented. We realize that some people may disagree with our approach, but we feel it made a stronger book.

Our selection criteria included lake size, configuration, and "wildness." As you read through our recommendations, you'll discover that bigger does not necessarily mean better, wildness does not necessarily require a remote location, and that many-branched lakes are usually more fun than round ones.

We also made a conscious effort to include some small lakes that are ideal for beginners or families with small children. Scotts Run Lake (twenty-one acres, Berks County), Laurel Lake (twenty-five acres, Cumberland County), Cowans Gap Lake (forty-two acres, Fulton County), Beaver Meadows Lake (fifty acres, Forest County), and Lyman Lake (forty-five acres, Potter County) all fit this description. There are great things to see at these lakes, but the lakes themselves are small enough that they won't intimidate beginners.

Our intent is to promote canoeing as a vehicle for wildlife watching—a means to more fully enjoy wildlife and nature. Physical challenge and the sheer joy of paddling are secondary. The real thrills come from close encounters with some of Earth's most magnificent creatures. Like the great egret we observed for forty-five minutes one day, never more than ten feet away. Or the white-tailed deer we came upon, standing knee-deep in the marsh we were exploring. Or the wood duck and her brood of thirteen downy ducklings, one of which was snatched from the watery depths even as we watched.

Planning Ahead

Before you set out on your Pennsylvania quiet water canoeing adventure, make sure you have the necessary resources. The *Pennsylvania Atlas and Gazetteer* provides detailed maps of every county and indicates secondary and unpaved roads, state parks, state forests, state game lands, and much more. It's not an infallible resource, but it's extremely helpful. Also, pick up brochures for the state parks you visit. These are available at the park office, and even though most park offices open at 8:00 A.M. and close at 4:00 P.M., the brochures are usually placed in a protected area outside, available at any time of the day or night. The brochures contain detailed maps of lakes, hiking trails, camping areas, and other facilities.

Another important consideration is to make sure your canoe is properly registered before you launch it in any Pennsylvania waterway. State residents must register their canoes with the Fish and Boat Commission and must display a state park launch permit to use any state park lake. Canoes registered in other states may use Pennsylvania waters, but they too must have a current state park launch permit to use state park lakes. Nonresidents who are not required to register their canoes in their home states must register their boats with the Fish and Boat Commission. For complete rules and regulations, an application, and fee structure, contact the Pennsylvania Fish and Boat Commission, P.O. Box 67000, Harrisburg, PA 17106-7000, stop in at any local Fish and Boat Commission office, or call 717-657-4540 for more information.

Safety First and Always

Federal and state law require that all vessels have on board a U.S. Coast Guard approved personal flotation device (PFD) for each person on board. For boats less than sixteen feet long and all canoes and kayaks, the PFD may be wearable or throwable. Though the law requires that PFDs need only be "readily accessible," we strongly recommend that everyone wear a PFD. At the very least, make this an absolute rule for all children under twelve and anyone who cannot swim.

A PFD may seem like a pain in the neck, but if ever you tip the canoe and bump your head, it can save your life.

Equipment

If you don't have a canoe but would like to give quiet water canoeing a try, you're in luck. Many Pennsylvania state parks rent canoes, paddles, and PFDs at reasonable rates. For a small investment you can take the entire family out for a day before spending any serious money.

If you've already decided that canoeing sounds like great outdoor fun, here's what you'll need: a canoe, a roof rack, paddles, PFDs, and water shoes. You can find all these items and a knowledgeable sales staff at most large outdoor equipment stores. And make sure to take a pair of binoculars. The excitement and thrill they'll add far outweigh the risk of getting them wet. Besides, you'd kick yourself if your first glimpse of a bald eagle or an osprey was just a speck on the other side of the lake.

There are many fine brands of canoes. Your best bet is to shop around and actually test-paddle different models to get a feel for how they handle. We bought a new seventeen-foot Coleman Ram-X 17 for this project. It proved to be extremely stable and maneuverable, well worth its modest price tag.

To transport a canoe, most folks use some sort of car roof rack. Metal racks that attach directly to the roof's rain gutters work best and are the most expensive route. We opted to use tightly ratcheted nylon straps and foam blocks to hold our canoe on the roof. Across more than 5,000 miles of Pennsylvania's highways and byways, this system worked well. However, be sure to check and tighten the straps periodically.

Paddles should fit the paddler and be comfortable. We used lightweight aluminum paddles tipped with tough plastic blades.

Coast Guard approved life preservers are widely available, inexpensive, and surprisingly comfortable. Buy ones that are designed to hold your head above water in case you lose consciousness. And be sure the PFD is the proper size for the person wearing it.

Comfortable water shoes are a must. When the water is low, someone's got to get out and pull the canoe to deeper water. And we've observed that most tipping accidents occur because most people are afraid to get their feet wet while they are getting in or out of the canoe. The simplest solution, at least during mild weather, is to wear water shoes that are expected to get wet. A cheap five-dollar pair of sneakers works as well as high-priced boat shoes.

Another piece of equipment that you might not automatically consider is an electric motor. Now, purists might object to putting a motor on a canoe, but after watching many motor-powered canoes making less noise than our paddles cruise by us, we don't think it's such a bad idea, especially if you plan to visit lakes larger than 250 acres. In fact, our next purchases will be a Coleman Scanoe, which is a square-sterned canoe, and an electric motor. Because electric motors are so quiet and emit no polluting waste, they are permitted on virtually any body of water in the state.

A few other items to carry along on every canoe trip include sunscreen, sunglasses, a big-brimmed hat, insect repellent, field guides, a compass, a water jug, and a lightweight cotton cover-up for when the sun gets too intense.

Technique

One of the big advantages quiet water canoeing has over other outdoor sports is that it requires little training. Anyone, young or old, can learn as they go. Beginners should start on small lakes where wind and waves are unlikely to be problems.

To paddle from the left side of the canoe, for example, grip the paddle with your left hand about twelve inches above the blade, as if shaking hands with it. Then clamp your right hand on the top of the paddle. Long, firm strokes with the blade completely submerged propel the canoe forward. To maintain a straight course, use the paddle as a rudder after every other stroke or push the paddle out after each stroke. To paddle from the right side, simply reverse your hands. To change directions, do a reverse stroke on the side of the canoe toward which you wish to turn. Those extremely basic instructions will get you started and moving. The rest is up to you.

To hone your paddling skills, take a few lessons, or consult any of these references: *Beyond the Paddle* (1991) by Garret Conover (Tilbury House), *Canoe* magazine and its annual *Beginners' Guide to Canoeing and Kayaking* (available on newsstands in April), and *L.L. Bean Guide to Canoeing* (video, 1985) with Ken Stone.

Timing Your Visits

What follows are the lakes, ponds, and reservoirs where we found the greatest opportunities to encounter wildlife, experience solitude, and enjoy nature. Keep in mind that your experience at any of these areas will vary greatly, depending upon your timing. The timing of a quiet water canoe trip is as important as location. Common sense would tell you that if you visit any Pennsylvania lake on a weekend between July 4 and Labor Day you're going to find other people there—and maybe lots of them. That's the nature of the state and its large, mobile population. But visit during a summer weekday or in the spring or fall, and you're likely to find yourself alone on some of the most beautiful lakes in the country.

Timing also includes time of day. An adventure in the early morning or early evening hours will be considerably different from a midday paddle. If wildlife watching is your goal, you'll canoe during the times of day when most species are active—morning and evening.

Then there are the seasons to consider. Spring and fall are when ducks, geese, and other migrating waterfowl visit the state's lakes in large numbers. Spring and early summer are generally best for seeing songbirds. Early June signals the bloom of the rhododendrons found so commonly in northern counties. Look for blooming water lilies, pickerelweed, and other common wetland species in summer. And while midsummer is not generally the greatest time to bird-watch, this is the time you'll begin seeing migrating shorebirds. Waters are generally low on many lakes in summer, exposing mudflats and sandbars, where the shorebirds love to feed. In September and October, enjoy the spectacular fall colors from the vantage point of a canoe on a lake ringed by steeply wooded slopes. There are also certain times and seasons to avoid, such as duck season on certain lakes in the fall or the opening day of trout season.

Getting There

We encourage you to enjoy your drive to these lakes and reservoirs. Pennsylvania scenery rivals any in the country. We found ourselves oohing and aahing a lot as we traveled across the state. We've included notes and information on things to watch for. And we've also included nearby points of interest whenever possible or appropriate.

Camping

Many canoeists also like to camp. The state has hundreds of thousands of acres of public lands, but little of it is open to campers. Many of the state parks include campsites, and we've indicated these. State park offices also keep lists of nearby private campgrounds. And camping is permitted in most areas of Allegheny National Forest. But camping is prohibited in state forests and state game lands, which account for the vast majority of public lands.

The Lake Ethic

Canoeists generally enjoy a good reputation as conservationists and careful stewards of the earth. Unfortunately, they must share the water with some people who aren't. We were discouraged by the Styrofoam bait containers, monofilament line, and beverage containers we found at some locations. The lakes managed by the Fish Commission seemed especially prone to attack by litterbugs.

We long for the day when everyone will be educated enough to clean up after themselves. In the meantime, we pick up trash whenever we can and try to leave each lake cleaner than we found it. We've observed other canoeists doing the same. Trash cans are available at most sites, except some Fish Commission lakes. But be prepared to carry out your recyclables. Only the state parks have recycling centers, and these are not always easily accessible or even complete (many don't take plastic, for example).

Beware of Deer

Finally, a few words about Pennsylvania's huge deer herd. It's possible to see deer at any of the sites we've listed; in many cases it's likely. You may even see them in the lakes, as we have on several occasions. But these same graceful animals that enhance your quiet water canoeing experience also pose a terrible menace on the state's roads and highways.

More than 43,000 deer were hit and killed by motorists on Pennsylvania highways in 1992, according to the most recent Game Commission count. And this doesn't even include the ones that manage to crawl off and die away from the highway, where they are not noticed or counted. Be extremely careful driving at dawn and dusk. And realize that when a deer jumps in front of your car, a second one is very often following close behind. Many people miss the first one and nail the second.

Enjoy!

We sincerely hope that you enjoy Pennsylvania's quiet waters as much as we do. You may have favorite lakes or discover new ones we haven't mentioned. Or perhaps you'll visit one of the large, unrestricted-use lakes and find a small branch perfect for canoeing. That's great! This book is only a "guide" to Pennsylvania's quiet water. Please write to us in care of AMC Books and tell us about your favorite places.

Like us, you will probably find that the difference between a lake you would recommend and revisit and one you thought disappointing is close encounters with wildlife. Most times, those magical wild moments occur on lakes with marshy areas and lots of hidden coves and inlets—on lakes undisturbed by powerboats and other recreational activities.

Happy canoeing!

Pennsylvania

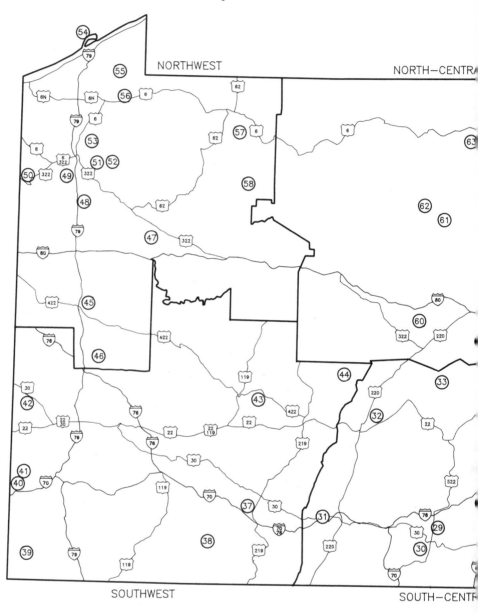

Note: See regional maps for the names of lakes numbered above:

Northeast Region	page 4	Southwest Region	page 110
Southeast Region	page 50	Northwest Region	page 136
South-Central Region	page 83	North-Central Region	page 182

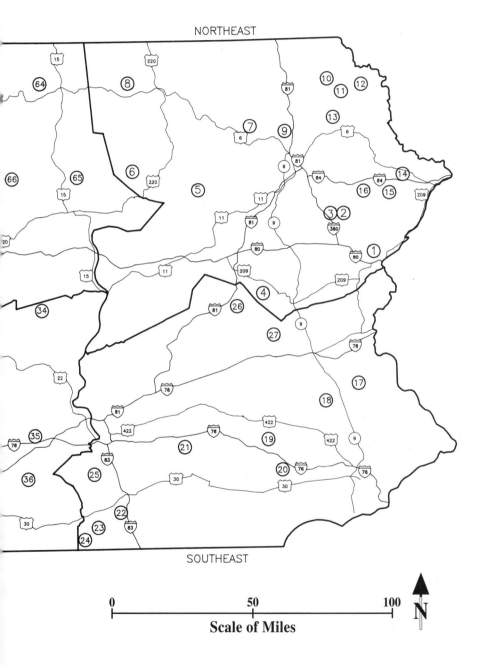

NORTHEAST

SOUTHEAST

0   50   100

Scale of Miles

N

Northeast Region

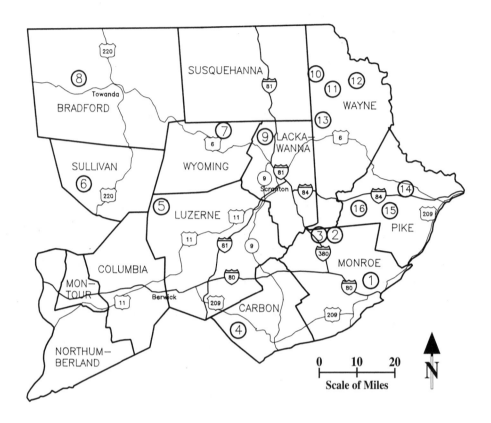

1. Bradys Lake
2. Tobyhanna Lake
3. Gouldsboro Lake
4. Mauch Chunk Lake
5. Lake Jean
6. Hunters Lake
7. Stevens Lake
8. Stephen Foster Lake
9. Lackawanna Lake

10. Belmont Lake
11. Miller Pond
12. Upper Woods Pond
13. White Oak Pond
14. Shohola Lake
15. Pecks Pond
16. Promised Land Lake
    and Lower Lake

Northeast Pennsylvania offers some of the most beautiful countryside in the state. The land is rocky and mountainous, and early pioneers toiled long and hard to clear the land of trees and rocks. The rocks they piled skillfully into long, straight walls that marked fields and property lines and kept livestock contained. These old walls are still very much in evidence around the entire region. They're a visual reminder of our connections to the past. In many places the old walls can be seen in the middle of a wooded area, signaling that what we view as a forest today was probably someone's homestead or farm field 150 years ago. The area also boasts many of the state's 221 covered bridges, located primarily in Columbia and Montour Counties.

The Pocono mountains dominate much of the northeast, and intense private development characterizes much of this popular vacation area. Today's vacation capital of Pennsylvania, the northeast historically witnessed the growth of America's coal and railroad industries in places such as Scranton and Wilkes-Barre. But there are still vast areas of public lakes and lands for all of us to enjoy, both in the Poconos and the Endless Mountains farther west.

There are more lakes in the northeast than in any other section of the state. In this section we've included the ones that best meet our requirements for a rewarding quiet water experience. We also briefly mention below a list of lakes that we didn't include, but that some canoeists might find interesting. Generally, these are larger recreational lakes with no restrictions on motor boating, or lakes close to large urban areas that are therefore more crowded, noisy, and less aesthetically appealing (to us, anyway). Under the right circumstances, though, you can enjoy quiet water canoe experiences on these lakes, too.

Lake Wallenpaupack, 5,700 acres bordering Pike and Wayne counties, was built and is maintained by the Pennsylvania Power and Light Company. It features four lakeshore campsites, each with its own launching area. High-powered recreational boats are permitted.

In Carbon County, the 949-acre Beltzville Lake is part of the 2,972-acre Beltzville State Park. Most types of recreational boats are permitted. The two eastern most branches of the lake above Preacher's Camp launch and Pine Run Cove are restricted to a "no wake" speed and are recommended for canoes and sailboats.

Frances Slocum Lake (165 acres) in Luzerne County's Frances Slocum State Park (1,035 acres) is limited to non-power and electric motors only. It's a pretty, U-shaped lake and well-suited for canoeing. But we discovered that its proximity to urban sprawl and its location right along a busy highway detract from the overall quiet water experience.

Bradys Lake

Size: 229 acres

RESTRICTIONS: nonpowered boats and electric motors only
MANAGING AGENCY: Fish and Boat Commission
LOCATION: near Blakeslee, Monroe County

Surrounded by state game lands, Bradys Lake offers refuge and seclusion in the crowded and overly developed Pocono Mountains. This fantastic lake features wooded shorelines characterized by birches, pines, and oaks. There's a small island in the southern portion, near the dam, covered with young birches and alder. The lake extends due north to its marshy upper end. We noticed three large beaver lodges along the west shore.

Toward the middle of the lake, both the east and west shorelines jut well into the water, almost cutting the lake in two, except for a

A great egret at Bradys Lake demonstrates the importance of quiet water canoeing for wildlife watching by staying within ten feet of the canoe for forty-five minutes.

The great egret snatches a dragonfly in midair and manipulates it in its huge bill before swallowing.

narrow channel. We had just cleared that channel on our way north when we noticed a white speck in the sedges along the eastern shore. With binoculars we identified it as a great egret—one of the few we've seen on Pennsylvania waters. We paddled steadily closer, hoping to get a better look and maybe a photo or two.

The bird was busily fishing among the bur-reeds (a type of sedge), and we approached it with ease. As it turned out, we spent about forty-five minutes with that bold bird, which stayed within fifteen feet of the canoe the entire time. And Scott shot four rolls of film! It was a defining moment of our quiet water canoe experience. At times we drifted within five feet of the great white bird.

We watched that proficient fisherman pull at least twelve minnows from the shallows, its long neck poised to strike like a snake. It simply swallowed each catch whole in one deft movement.

Suddenly, as we watched not ten feet away, a dragonfly approached. The egret cocked its head, and we could see its eyes follow the dragonfly's line of flight. Then, quick as lightning—so quick that Scott missed the shot, even though he was looking through the camera's viewfinder, with his finger on the release—the big bird snatched the dragonfly from the air. The dragonfly struggled, its membranous wings chattering, but the egret kept that long bill clamped shut. Finally, the struggling subsided, and the egret swallowed its victim. A "fly-catching" egret was a new one for us.

The egret fished and fished, and we watched and watched. Shortly after the dragonfly incident, the bird speared a good-sized minnow. The fishing technique was quite different this time. The egret crouched down, quivered like a cat stalking its prey, then struck. It actually impaled the fish on its lower bill. The fish struggled, so it took the egret some time and finesse to work the fish off its lower bill and head first into its gullet. But in less than a minute, the egret was stalking prey again.

So absorbed were we in this incredible wildlife encounter that we hadn't noticed the darkening sky. Suddenly the wind picked up, and a storm blew in. The lake's upper end was not far away, and the temptation to continue into that marshy, tree-stump-studded area almost overwhelmed us. Fortunately, good sense prevailed. We hightailed it south toward the launch and lost Linda's cap in the process. High wind on a body of water that size can create some serious whitecaps.

We regretted not making it all the way to the lake's north end. But we've already made plans to return to Bradys Lake.

GETTING THERE: From the northeast extension of the Pennsylvania Turnpike, take Exit 35 and get on I-80 East. Take Exit 43 (Blakeslee) and head north on Route 115 for 1.3 miles. Turn right (east) onto Route 940. Go 5.1 miles, turn left at a small, obscure lake sign on access road. Drive 3.5 miles to launch.

Tobyhanna Lake

Size: 170 acres

RESTRICTIONS: nonpowered boats and electric motors only
MANAGING AGENCY: Tobyhanna State Park (5,440 acres)
LOCATION: near Tobyhanna, Monroe County

During the first part of the twentieth century, Tobyhanna Lake and nearby Gouldsboro Lake supported thriving ice industries. Ice cut from the lakes and stored during the winter later kept produce and meats fresh as they were shipped by railway to East Coast cities. Ice from these lakes even made its way to Florida to be used in hospitals.

Today, ice still plays a dominant role at Tobyhanna. Many people visit this lake in the winter for ice fishing and ice skating. And the lake's a popular summer recreation spot as well.

Tobyhanna Lake lies in a southwest to northeast orientation, narrowing in the north, where Tobyhanna Creek leaves its swampy environs to enter the lake. The entire lake can be explored in a few leisurely hours, but two areas deserve special attention.

The first is a large cove along the northwest shore. Here, where Pole Bridge Run enters the lake, sits a large beaver lodge. There is a lot of other beaver evidence, and when the water is high enough in the spring, it's possible to paddle up into the run a short way. Emergent tree stumps and wood duck boxes give this cove a lived-in look. We didn't see any wood ducks, but a great blue heron fished the shallows, watching us warily.

Along the north shore of this cove lie some beautiful, wooded campsites. There is a separate launch site here just for campers, but park office employees told us it was okay to launch a canoe right from a lakeside campsite. (It requires just a short portage.) Blueberry bushes abound here, and during the July blueberry season, many campers fill pails with berries. The black bears love them, too. Park rangers told us campers could expect to see bears in the campgrounds every night, drawn even more by carelessly stored human food than the naturally occurring berries.

The second area ripe for canoe explorations is the marshy headwaters of Tobyhanna Creek at the lake's northern end. "Tobyhanna" is a Native American name meaning "stream whose banks are fringed with alder." And indeed, the area north of the lake, drained by the creek, is swampy and characterized by alders and other wetland species. Barring a summer drought, it's possible to paddle upstream into this swampy area. You can't reach the creek from the lake—the park road to the campground cuts off the access—but just past the bridge is Parking Lot #5. From here, you can put in at the north end of the parking lot, if you don't mind wading through some vegetation first. Park employees told us birders often canoe this biologically rich area.

The southern portion of the lake is pretty, too. The shorelines are primarily wooded with beech, birch, maple, and some pine. There's a swimming beach, a boat rental concession, and a public boat launch along the eastern shore.

For more information, call the park office at 717-894-8336 or 8337.

GETTING THERE: From I-380, take Tobyhanna exit (No. 7) and travel north on Route 423 for 2.5 miles to the boat launch on the left.

Gouldsboro Lake
Size: 250 acres

RESTRICTIONS: nonpowered boats and electric motors only
MANAGING AGENCY: Gouldsboro State Park (2,800 acres)
LOCATION: near Gouldsboro, Monroe County

When we studied the state park map showing Gouldsboro Lake, we saw a basically oval lake running north to south, with a few small coves on the west shore and an interesting crooked finger cutting into the east shore. Nice, but probably not terribly exciting, we thought.

But maps can deceive. We discovered that the south end of the lake is a maze of small islands and emergent stumps. Canoeing this area, especially on a windy day, tests the maneuvering skills of even veteran paddlers. Twice we came close to swamping here when we ran aground on submerged logs. The tendency is to try and shimmy and shake yourself forward, pushing and pulling with the paddles. But fight the urge. Calmly back up by paddling backward or pushing off the log. Avoid swinging one end of the canoe parallel with the log. This is where you become most unstable and most likely to tip. That day at Gouldsboro, each time we hit a submerged log, the wind blew the back end of our canoe around until we were almost parallel with the log. It was pretty tense, but we managed to escape upright each time.

On a calmer day we would have taken the time to appreciate the "rafts" of plant life found all over the lake's southern end. From almost every emergent log and tree stump, green growth sprouted and thrived, forming these "rafts" of vegetation. The vegetation, in turn, is home to many different insects. As these logs and stumps rot, they provide a very rich humus for plant growth. Seeds borne on the wind, in duck droppings, or by other animals wind up on the logs, where they sprout. And voilà, a new biotic community begins.

Vegetative rafts are wonderful to study and photograph. But they are less enjoyable to maneuver around in gusty winds. After dodging the obstacle course for awhile, we beached our canoe and explored one of the larger islands. It was covered with blueberry bushes. We ate our fill, sharing the bushes with cedar waxwings, also gorging themselves. We continued our island exploration, startling a young cottontail and several Canada geese in the process.

Other animals commonly seen in the park area include black bears, beavers, raccoons, snowshoe hares, mink, foxes, deer, and muskrats.

A watercraft concession rents canoes and sailboats during the summer. There's also a swimming beach along the western shore, north of the boat launch. The park also features picnic areas and miles of hiking trails. The Frank Gantz Trail, accessible from the boat launch parking area, encircles the lake's southern end, then heads east into Tobyhanna State Park and Black Bear Swamp, where it connects with Lakeside Trail and eventually leads to Tobyhanna Lake itself. There are no campsites at Gouldsboro State Park, but 140 beautifully wooded, primitive, year-round campsites can be found in the nearby Tobyhanna State Park.

For more information call the park office at 717-894-8336 or 8337.

GETTING THERE: From I-380, take Exit 6 (Gouldsboro, Route 507) and head east on Route 507 for 1.9 miles. Turn right at park sign onto State Park Road. Drive 1.7 miles to launch.

Mauch Chunk Lake

Size: 345 acres

RESTRICTIONS: nonpowered boats and electric motors only
MANAGING AGENCIES: Mauch Chunk Lake Park and Fish and
   Boat Commission
LOCATION: near Jim Thorpe, Carbon County

Mauch Chunk Lake offers the opportunity for a great aerobic workout
in your canoe. Not many lakes of this size and configuration are limited
to electric motors. Even sailboat size is restricted to seventeen feet.
There are no real coves or inlets, just a long, straight lake that extends
about 2.8 miles from its dam in the east to its marshy west end. The
lake is sandwiched between Mauch Chunk Ridge along the south shore
and Pisgah Mountain to the north. Both the lake and the nearby town of
Mauch Chunk (now called Jim Thorpe) were named after Mauch
Chunk Ridge, which is a Native American name meaning "sleeping
bear." The native residents of the area thought the ridge viewed from
afar resembled a large, sleeping bear.

The south shoreline is completely wooded and undeveloped, while
the north shoreline features rhododendron and laurel thickets, fields,
hemlock stands, and a few deciduous woodlots. On the north shore
there are launches at the east and west ends (both open twenty-four
hours, year-round), a swimming beach, camping sites, picnic pavilions,
and a boat rental concession. Wooded tent sites can accommodate families or groups. An environmental education center, located near the
west end, offers interpretive exhibits and programs.

Another important feature of the park's 2,100 acres is the various
hiking trails through natural and historic areas. A 1.5-mile Shoreline
Trail allows visitors to guide themselves (with the help of a self-inter-
pretive brochure) through open shoreline, deciduous woods, rhododendron and laurel thickets, and hemlock stands. The Woods Trail leads to
the lake's marshy and swampy west end. The 3.5-mile Fireline Trail
extends along the Mauch Chunk Ridge, through oak forest. And the
Switchback Trail travels along a former gravity railroad, which brought
coal down the mountain from Summit Hill to Jim Thorpe.

Mauch Chunk Lake hosts numerous migrating waterfowl, so your
best bet for wildlife watching (and fewer people) would be a spring or
fall visit.

NEARBY: If you visit this lake, plan time to also visit the Victorian town of Jim Thorpe, which is only four miles east. Built in the nineteenth century by coal barons, the town features beautifully restored homes, antique shops, galleries, and boutiques nestled on a mountainside. It's known as the "Switzerland of America." Originally called Mauch Chunk, the town now takes its name from the famous Native American athlete who won Olympic gold medals in 1912 in the pentathlon and decathlon. Curiously, Thorpe never even lived in the town now named for him. Descended from both the Sauk and Fox tribes, he spent the early years of his life in Oklahoma, then attended the Carlisle (PA) Indian School as a teenager. The town's renaming had more to do with public relations and trying to revive a sagging local economy than with any ties Thorpe had to the area.

We were fortunate enough to spend a night at The Inn at Jim Thorpe, a lovely Victorian inn with all the comforts of today. The inn accommodates outdoor-lovers of all types, even providing storage for mountain bikes and early morning breakfasts for canoeists who want to beat the crowds and the sun. For information, call 717-325-2599.

GETTING THERE: From the only stoplight in historic downtown Jim Thorpe (near The Inn), take Broadway west for four miles. (Outside of town, Broadway becomes the Lentz Trail Highway.) Turn left at the park sign to the first launch. Or, continue another two miles on Lentz Trail Highway to a second launch.

Dragonflies and Damselflies

Though it's sometimes true we don't see the forest for the trees, it's also true that we sometimes miss the trees for the forest. Whenever we canoe a lake, for example, we focus our attention on birds, turtles, fish, or the water itself. But just above the surface, on logs, cattails, and emergent rocks, live some of the most common members of any wetland community—dragonflies and damselflies.

The dragonflies and damselflies, members of the insect order Odonata, make fascinating subjects for nature watchers. They are relatively large, easy to see, active all day long, and confine their territorial activities to a small area. Many are brightly colored and strikingly marked.

We've all seen them, up close and personal. On family canoe outings, my daughters love to hold their arms out and sit still.

It's not long until a damselfly perches on their arms or heads.

The basic body plan for these insects is similar—a large head dominated by huge compound eyes, lacy transparent wings, and an elongated body. Dragonflies are larger, have stouter bodies, and, at rest, hold their wings flat and perpendicular to the body. Damselflies, as the name suggests, are more delicate. They have much slimmer bodies and, at rest, hold their wings together over the body.

Though they are predators and look ferocious, dragonflies and damselflies pose no harm to people. They do not sting, but larger dragonflies can bite if handled. The sensation, however, is nothing more than a pinch. They patrol wetlands and even nearby fields and woodlots in search of prey. Sometimes they hunt from a perch; sometimes they hunt on the wing. In either case, their huge compound eyes enable them to spot small flying insects—flies, gnats, mosquitoes—while flying.

Dragonflies and damselflies attack by air. Powered by two pairs of powerful and maneuverable membranous wings, they use their legs to capture prey. Their legs are covered with spines, and when they are held just right, they form a basket or net into which they funnel their victims. After capturing their prey in the feeding "basket," they either eat it on the wing or rest on a perch and enjoy a leisurely meal.

Next time you get to the water's edge, make it a point to spend just ten or fifteen minutes watching the dragonflies. Observe how they hunt. Also notice their fiercely territorial behavior. Male dragonflies and damselflies defend small pieces of space just as birds do. When not hunting, they spend most of their time perching, patrolling, and crisscrossing the territory watching for intruders. While perched, they vigilantly scan the territory for intruders. If another male approaches, the resident male gives chase. Usually the intruder leaves, but sometimes there is a fight accompanied by a noisy clash of wings. Other times the rivals hover, face each other, and perform an aerial dance. The outcome of these ritualized matchups determines which individual is dominant.

The reward of dominance is access to females for mating. When a female visits an occupied territory, the dominant male mates with her. That's what's going on during those familiar acrobatic wrestling matches in which the male grasps the female from above. After mating, the female hovers just above the surface of the water and lays eggs on floating leaves or on rocks just below the surface. About a week later, the eggs hatch and the nymphs drift to the bottom, where they assume their role as fierce underwater predators. Dragonflies may live in the nymph stage for several years before transforming into adults. Damselflies usually emerge as adults the following year.

When the time comes to transform into the adult stage, the nymphs climb out of the water onto a piece of emergent vegetation. Before the nymph can dry out, its exoskeleton splits down the back, and an adult dragonfly or damselfly emerges. The adult rests for several hours while blood pumps through and unfurls its wings. As soon as the wings dry out and harden, the contests for territories, dominance, and females begin. Adults live for only a few weeks, but because nymphs emerge and transform into adults all summer long, dragonflies and damselflies are always abundant.

As you paddle Pennsylvania's waters, watch for several common species. Short-tailed damselflies are probably the most common member of this group of insects. You'll find them anywhere you find quiet water. They are easily recognized by their bright blue body with several black bands that encircle the abdomen. They are also called bluets.

Among dragonflies, the skimmers are a large group that includes many species with bold black or orange marks on clear membranous wings. We've seen white-tailed skimmers (males have a chalky white abdomen) on virtually every lake we've canoed. The darners include the state's largest dragonflies. Most are blue or green, and the largest species can measure more than three inches long. The green darner, like the monarch butterfly but unlike most other insects, migrates. It travels between breeding grounds in Pennsylvania and wintering areas farther south.

Dragonflies and damselflies offer quiet water canoeists compelling action regardless of the time of day. When the fish aren't biting or the birds are quiet, just float to the shore and enjoy the odonates. It's a show that plays all day, every day, all summer long.

Lake Jean
Size: 245 acres

RESTRICTIONS: nonpowered boats and electric motors only
MANAGING AGENCY: Rickett's Glen State Park (13,050 acres)
LOCATION: near Red Rock, Luzerne County

Rickett's Glen State Park is a sentimental favorite with us. This is where, a long time ago, we became engaged to be married. Like most visitors, we were first drawn here by the magnificent spectacle of twenty-two waterfalls cascading down a mountainside. More recently, we've come to appreciate the park's other main attraction—Lake Jean.

Lake Jean covers a large area, and canoeists can easily spend a half day or more exploring its waters and shoreline. From its dam at the south end, the lake branches north, then curves east in a wide U shape. Many little islands cluster around the western side of the U. These are fun to maneuver around and are popular with boaters and canoeists.

West of the islands, where the lake turns sharply south, the shoreline is covered with highbush blueberries. There's a campground on this peninsula, and when we beached here to pick blueberries we found many campers doing the same thing. Walking inland a ways just to

Midweek is the best time to visit Lake Jean at Rickett's Glen State Park.

Though we only saw one wind-powered "sail-canoe" all summer, this one on Lake Jean sure looks like fun.

stretch our legs a bit, we found three fawns, each visiting a different campsite. One actually was eating out of a woman's hand. Earlier we had seen a doe and two fawns standing along the park road, posing for visitors' cameras.

It was also just off this peninsula that we saw another interesting sight: a canoeist who had rigged up a sail on his canoe. He also had a rudder, stabilizers on either side, and a little chair for himself. He attracted a lot of attention as he whisked by those of us paddling.

Lake Jean's shoreline and the surrounding park feature a rich diversity of trees. This part of the state is a meeting ground for northern and southern hardwood species.

Finally, no visit to Lake Jean would be complete without experiencing the park's primary scenic attraction—the Glens Natural Area, a National Natural Landmark. Here, two branches of Kitchen Creek, the lake's feeder stream, cut through deep gorges, creating more than twenty-two waterfalls. The highest is 94-foot Ganoga Falls. The two creek branches eventually meet to flow through Rickett's Glen. Trails parallel each stream. Many visitors enjoy hiking down one stream and back up along the other. It's an ancient and magical land. The wooded trails cut through stands of giant pines, oaks, and hemlocks, many towering over 100 feet high, with diameters up to 5 feet. Park literature reports that many of these trees have been standing more than 500 years. Ring counts on fallen trees show ages of up to 900 years.

The park also offers 120 campsites and ten modern cabins open year-round. There's a swimming beach and boat rental concession at the east end of Lake Jean. This is a breathtakingly beautiful, but popular, park. We'd suggest you avoid the area on summer weekends.

For more information, call the park office at 717-477-5675.

GETTING THERE: From I-80 in Bloomsburg, take Exit 35 and head north on Route 487 for about thirty miles. This road leads directly to the park. However, the last four miles of this route are extremely steep and should be avoided if you are pulling heavy trailer units. Instead, approach the park on Route 487 south from Dushore.

Hunters Lake

Size: 117 acres

RESTRICTIONS: nonpowered boats and electric motors only
MANAGING AGENCY: Fish and Boat Commission
LOCATION: near Eagles Mere, Sullivan County

Located in a remote mountainous area, Hunters Lake is a good excuse for a scenic backcountry drive. Engulfed by Wyoming State Forest, the lake offers spectacular views of the surrounding mountains. The lake itself is narrow and reaches at least three-quarters of a mile from its dam at the south end to a concrete walkway extending across the entire north end. The wooded shoreline boasts just a fringe of bur-reed and cut-grass.

Despite its remoteness, there were a surprising number of fishermen there the summer Saturday we visited. We didn't see as much wildlife as we had hoped, but the mountain views more than compensated for the wildlife. After a brisk paddle from the launch to the dam and back to the north end, we floated leisurely south to the launch, drinking in the mountain air and mountain views. During a weekday or in the spring or fall, you could probably expect to be pretty much alone on this lake.

At the lake's north end, we took some time to examine the flowering pickerelweed. This plant has a bad reputation because it chokes waterways and small ponds. But it's a lovely plant. Common along the edges of ponds, this plant stands eighteen to thirty inches tall. Its flower stem emerges from a sheath just below a large, arrowhead-shaped leaf that's four to six inches long. Its "flower" is actually a spike of many small, purple flowers. Each flower's two lips is three-lobed; the center upper lobe has two bright spots to attract the attention of pollinators (bees, flies, etc.). The flowers are aromatic but not fragrant. The plant stalk is fibrous and difficult to break. And note the swirled configuration of veins on the leaves.

Take some time to drive along the forest service roads near the lake. State forests are public property and are there for all of us to use. They cover more than 2 million acres and include some of the most scenic spots and isolated trout fishing streams in the commonwealth. Graded gravel or paved roads provide access for those who don't have the time or physical ability to hike the numerous trails and old logging roads crisscrossing the state's forests. Just make sure you have a good

Pickerelweed is one of the most abundant emergent aquatic plants found along the edges of Pennsylvania lakes.

map along. Roads and trails are not always well marked, and it's easy to get lost. The *Pennsylvania Atlas and Gazetteer* (DeLorme Mapping Company) provides good information on state forest roads. But for the most detailed and accurate information on roads, trails, topography, and more, get a map of the individual state forest you plan to visit. Maps of all the state forests are available from the Department of Environmental Resources, Bureau of Forestry, P.O. Box 8552, Harrisburg, PA 17105-8552.

GETTING THERE: From U.S. 220 at Muncy Valley, take Route 42 north for 2.6 miles. Bear left onto Brunnerdale Road and go 0.7 mile to the launch.

Stevens Lake

Size: 62 acres

RESTRICTIONS: nonpowered boats and electric motors only
MANAGING AGENCY: Fish and Boat Commission
LOCATION: near Lemon, Wyoming County

This pretty little lake extends northwest from its dam at the south end. The shoreline is mostly wooded, except for a small open area and house at the south end. A small, roundish peninsula juts into the water in front of the dam, and here we found evidence of an old beaver lodge. The pointed, gnawed ends of the thick, weathered tree branches and twigs were a sure sign of beavers, but the pile they had apparently once formed was breaking apart and sinking.

Dense beds of yellow water lilies choke the northwest end. We had fun paddling the channels cutting through these lily beds. We never see much action among lily pads, so we decided to stop paddling and just observe for awhile. It was a cool but sunny day, and it felt good to sit and "thermoregulate."

The only things moving were the white-tailed skimmers—a common pond dragonfly with a broad, dark band across the middle of each wing and a white abdomen. (Females have spotted wings and a dark abdomen.) Suddenly, a largemouth bass shattered the stillness as it propelled itself up through the lily pads. Almost faster than we could register, it snatched a skimmer and crashed back into the water. The split-second incident startled us so badly that we seriously rocked the canoe.

Paddling back to the launch, we dodged emergent tree stumps and admired the thick clumps of pickerelweed along the shoreline. A domestic goose, honking loudly, spotted us from across the lake and swam hard to intercept us. It followed us all the way to the launch, even leaving the water when we did. It seemed edgy and not quite friendly, as if we'd invaded its personal property. We decided it was the Stevens Lake guard goose.

GETTING THERE: From U.S. 6 in Tunkhannock, take Route 29 north for 4.2 miles, turn left at the lake sign onto Lakewood Road (just past bridge), and go 0.1 mile. Turn right at sign onto dirt access road and launch.

Stephen Foster Lake

Size: 75 acres

RESTRICTIONS: nonpowered boats and electric motors only
MANAGING AGENCY: Mt. Pisgah State Park (1,302 acres)
LOCATION: near Burlington, Bradford County

Named for the famous American composer who once lived nearby, Stephen Foster Lake provides a friendly, easy lake for beginning canoeists or those with children who want to paddle. From its dam at the east end, the lake curves gently southwest. In the southwest corner, one arm extends northwest, severed from the main body of the lake by State Park Road. This marshy area is not accessible from the lake and has no separate launch of its own, but the Mill Stream Nature Trail leads along its southern shore. It's a great place to stretch canoe-stiff legs and observe red-winged blackbirds, herons, and other bird and insect life.

The lake's south shoreline is wooded, while a swimming pool, boat rental concession, and picnic pavilions cover much of the north shore. A marshy area just west of the dam teems with a variety of dragonflies and damselflies. The lake is big enough to offer some challenge and change of scenery but small enough and developed enough so that canoes and other watercraft are always nearby.

Surrounded by Mt. Pisgah State Park, the lake lies in the Endless Mountains region, located in the state's scenic northern tier. Eleven miles of hiking trails provide access to the woods and old farm fields comprising the park. The Oh! Susanna Trail circles the lake and is an easy trail for younger children. More challenging is the steep Ridge Trail, which leads to the Mt. Pisgah County Park west of the lake. Scenic overlooks reward those who venture here. Evening fell before we had a chance to hike this trail, but we'll catch it on our next trip. Mill Stream Nature Trail starts at State Park Road in the southwest corner of the lake and heads northwest toward Mill Creek, the lake's feeder stream.

A visitor's center highlights area wildlife and the early farm life of the New England pioneers who settled this area. The center features old farm implements recovered when the state park was developed in the 1970s. The visitor's center, open from Memorial Day through Labor Day, schedules weekend nature programs and nature day camps for children.

Although no camping is permitted on-site, campers are welcome at the nearby Mt. Pisgah County Park. However, no water or facilities are available except pit toilets. For information on nearby private campgrounds with full facilities or more information about the area, call the park office at 717-297-2734.

NEARBY: The newly created Bradford County Farm Museum in Troy, nine miles west of the lake on U.S. 6, showcases old farm equipment of all types. Permanent displays include an 1800s farm kitchen, a doctor's office, and a harness shop. Other exhibits change periodically.

Adjoining the state park south of the lake is State Game Land No. 289. This 1,552-acre tract, like the rest of the Game Commission's 1,221,000 acres, is open to hikers, bird-watchers, and other nature lovers. Simply obey posted rules and regulations, and do not enter marked wildlife refuges and propagation areas.

GETTING THERE: From U.S. 6 in West Burlington, between Troy and Towanda, head north on S.R. 3019 at park sign. Go 2.6 miles, turn right at park sign on S.R. 4015, and go 1 mile to park office. Continue past the office to the boat launch at the lake's east end, near the dam.

Lackawanna Lake

Size: 210 acres

RESTRICTIONS: nonpowered boats and electric motors only
MANAGING AGENCY: Lackawanna State Park (1,411 acres)
LOCATION: near Wallsville, Lackawanna County

Located just ten miles northeast of Scranton, Lackawanna Lake and State Park see heavy use, especially in the summer. But the interestingly shaped lake offers a fun canoeing adventure and plenty to see along its 7.5 miles of shoreline. Long and narrow, the lake looks like a capital letter J. The top of the J faces south, and the rest of the lake extends north about 2.5 miles. The southwest shoreline is well developed for day use and camping, but woods surround most of the remaining shoreline, with some overgrown pastures and a marshy north end.

We launched from the middle of the lake, just south of the Route 407 bridge, and headed south into a marshy cove on the east side. This cove curves around to the south and provides a private haven for watching kingfishers, herons, and ducks. Farther south is a large arm extending east about a quarter of a mile. (This is the top of the J.)

Great blue herons stand five feet tall. They are common on Pennsylvania's quiet water.

As we approached this great blue heron at Lackawanna Lake, it flew right in front of our canoe.

Heading north again, we paddled under the Route 407 bridge and entered Kennedy Creek, a feeder stream that enters on the east side. This creek is perfect for canoes. Even though the water level was low, we paddled upstream at least a quarter mile. Pines and hemlocks line the shore of this quiet and densely wooded stretch. We watched a muskrat along the shore, eating aquatic vegetation.

Bullhead Bay, north of the Kennedy Creek inlet, is another marshy cove. This must be a fishing hot spot for great blue herons, for we saw three here, fishing individually about 100 yards apart. Solitary by nature, great blues rarely congregate. From Bullhead Bay east, toward the bottom of the J, the lake narrows and becomes marshy. Water level determines how far you can paddle. This end of the lake is far less popular with park visitors. We encountered one fisherman and two white-tailed deer during our visit.

The park also has a swimming pool, boat rental concession, a ninety-six-site campground, and more than five miles of hiking trails.

For more information, call the park office at 717-945-3239 or the campground office at 717-563-9995.

NEARBY: Archibald Pothole State Park, site of the world's largest glacial pothole, is just southeast of Lackawanna Lake and northeast of

Scranton, off U.S. 6. This natural funnel-shaped formation is thirty-eight feet deep, forty-two feet across at the surface, and sixteen feet across at the bottom. Discovered by miners in 1884, the pothole was formed about 15,000 years ago when a stream cut through a glacier, creating a whirlpool above a natural depression in the underlying rock. Over time, the whirling motion of the stream's sand, gravel, and rock fragments cut through sandstone, shale, and coal to form the pothole. The park, which is a picnic and day-use area, is a satellite of Lackawanna State Park. For information, call the park office number listed above.

Some twenty-five miles to the northwest of Lackawanna State Park is Salt Springs State Park, another satellite park. The park features waterfalls and virgin hemlock stands. For information, call Lackawanna State Park.

GETTING THERE: From I-81 north of Scranton, take Exit 60 and head west on Route 524. Go 3.3 miles, then turn north on Route 407. Go 0.3 mile, turn left after bridge, and make another quick left to launch. There is another launch off Rt. 438 at the northern tip of the lake and another off Route 407 at the southern tip.

Great Blue Country

Midday is probably the worst time to paddle a lake during the summer months. The sun glares bright and hot, and there's not much to see. Unless you hug the shoreline and watch for motion. That's where you'll find great blue herons whiling away the day. And if you're lucky, you may spot one fishing. Watch for sudden movements. The heron's long neck fires and recoils in the blink of an eye, stabbing the surface of the quiet water. If you're quick with your binoculars, you'll get to watch the stately great blue flip a minnow into the air and swallow it whole.

Found along virtually every waterway in North America, great blues often escape detection despite their five-foot-tall profile. Sometimes they perch motionless, high in a tree on the water's edge. More often, they stand quietly in the shallows, scanning the water for fish. As fish approach, the heron freezes. When a fish swims within reach, the long powerful neck explodes to full extension. In an instant, the strike is complete.

A great blue grabs small fish crosswise, using its bill like a tweezers, then lifts its head and finesses the fish until it can be swallowed headfirst. Larger fish likewise are swallowed headfirst but are caught by being impaled on the heron's long pointed bill. The advantage of swallowing fish headfirst is to prevent fin bones from impaling the heron's throat.

Great blues are most often seen flying overhead. The seven-foot wingspan, slow wing beats, neck drawn back in an S curve, and long legs trailing behind the body make them easy to recognize. The blue-gray body and black-and-white neck and head are usually lost in silhouette.

Many people see these tall, long-legged birds and call them cranes or storks. In fact, I get calls to that effect several times each year. But cranes and storks rarely visit Pennsylvania. In parts of the country where cranes and storks dwell, there's an easy way to tell them apart. Cranes and storks fly with their necks extended. Herons (and egrets, for that matter) fly with their necks pulled back in that S shaped position.

If you watch a heron hunt, you'll notice that many strikes are unsuccessful. Like any other frustrated fisherman, a great blue will eventually walk or glide to another spot. A heron's hunting success ranges from twenty-five to fifty percent. That may not

seem too impressive at first. But consider that a baseball player who gets a base hit thirty percent of the time is Hall of Fame material. If an angler caught a fish every three or four casts, he (or she) would never stop fishing.

Despite the great blue's attraction to water, its diet is not limited to fish. It also eats frogs, snakes, crayfish, insects, shrimp, crabs, and even mice, shrews, and small rats. The varied diet may make feeding young herons a bit more manageable, especially in dry years.

Unlike many birds, great blue herons are communal nesters— they nest in colonies, often great distances from feeding areas. It is not uncommon for herons to fly ten, twenty, or even thirty miles to a feeding area each day. One of the largest rookeries (nesting colonies) in Pennsylvania is the Brucker Great Blue Heron Sanctuary in Mercer County just off Route 18 between Greenville and Sharon. The herons return each year in late February or early March, and by the peak of the nesting season later in the spring, as many as 200 nests are active.

Both great blue parents take turns incubating the four or five eggs for about twenty-eight days during late spring. Newly hatched young remain in the nest for two to three months before fledging.

An active rookery can get crowded and noisy. Each tree

may hold several nests and a dozen or more young birds. Fortunately, rookeries are usually in remote woodlands where detection by humans is unlikely. In fact, in Pennsylvania, many rookeries are located in remote mountainous areas. One in Clinton County sits atop a 2,000-foot-high plateau more than ten miles from a suitable feeding area.

Great blue herons linger in the area well into the fall—as long as there's ice-free water to fish in. During mild winters they may stay all year.

Next time you paddle around a lake or drive along a stream or river, keep your eyes peeled for sudden movement. You're in great blue country.

Belmont Lake

Size: 172 acres

RESTRICTIONS: nonpowered boats and electric motors only
MANAGING AGENCY: Fish and Boat Commission
LOCATION: near Pleasant Mount, Wayne County

Wooded Belmont Lake offers an escape from summer crowds. It's a long ways from anywhere, but the peace and solitude here are well worth the drive. Early on a midsummer morning we watched three bucks in velvet emerge from the woods near the boat launch and come for a drink at water's edge. They weren't at all worried by our canoe. We watched as they walked along the west shore for several minutes.

From its dam at the south end, Belmont Lake runs north, curves east, then heads north again. The lakeshore is completely wooded. On the east shore, the trees meet the water. But along the west shore, a marshy fringe of sedges, willows, and birch saplings lies between the woods and the water. Emergent stumps dot the waters, concentrated mainly at the north end. We watched a great blue heron fish from one close to the shore.

A beaver lodge sat at the southwest corner of the lake, but the water level was so low that the lodge was completely exposed. No doubt the beaver had moved on. At a huge rock that juts out from the east shore, we moored our canoe and climbed out to bird-watch. Scott whistles like a screech owl to attract songbirds, and that morning it really worked—eight species mobbed us in just five minutes!

Belmont Lake is not on the way to anywhere, and there's no place nearby to camp. But it's a beautiful, isolated lake reached via a scenic drive through northeast Pennsylvania's rolling hills. We recommend a visit. This lake, combined with Miller Pond just six miles away, would make a pleasant day of quiet water canoeing. And the fall colors here would be spectacular, as hills ring the lake.

NEARBY: Brown's Country Corner, a general store and restaurant in Pleasant Mount, along Route 670, offers plain but delicious home-cooked food. And it's a good thing, because eateries are few and far between in this region. Try the giant cheeseburger on a kaiser roll!

GETTING THERE: From U.S. 6 in Honesdale, take Route 670 North for 16.7 miles. Turn right (still on Route 670 North) at lake sign and go another 2.3 miles. Turn right at lake sign onto access road.

Miller Pond

Size: 61 acres

RESTRICTIONS: nonpowered boats and electric motors only
MANAGING AGENCY: Fish and Boat Commission
LOCATION: near Pleasant Mount, Wayne County

When we first saw Miller Pond, we were struck by the preponderance of birch trees along its shore. Soon, our eyes were drawn to the north shore, where the birches all leaned heavily to the east. This, no doubt, is the result of strong westerly winds and the species' tendency to bend under the slightest pressure. Remembering Robert Frost's poem from high school, we both had the same thought, and smiled as we expressed it in unison: "One could do worse than be a swinger of birches."

Miller Pond is basically oval shaped. The dam is located at the south end. The eastern shore is marshy, and buttonbush abounds in the shallow waters just offshore. One of the most common wetland shrubs, buttonbush stems have opposite leaves and small, white flowers clustered in ball-like heads. The shrub blooms later in summer, filling the air with a strong fragrance. The seeds produced by the buttonbush float on water, drifting to other parts of a lake or pond. In winter, the seeds provide food for ducks.

A botanically diverse island at the lake's southern tip, beside the dam, captured most of our interest. We spent a fair amount of time identifying such species as common arrowhead, bittersweet nightshade, arrow arum, cattails, leatherleaf, joe-pyeweed, alder, honeysuckle, wild iris, pickerelweed, and many more.

We'd recommend combining a visit to Miller Pond with a trip to Belmont Lake, only six miles west.

GETTING THERE: From Pleasant Mount at the junction of Routes 670 and 371, proceed east on Route 371 for 3.7 miles. Turn right onto S.R. 4029 at sign for lake. Go 1.7 miles, then turn left onto access road at launch site.

Upper Woods Pond

Size: 90 acres

RESTRICTIONS: nonpowered boats and electric motors only
MANAGING AGENCY: Fish and Boat Commission and Game Commission
LOCATION: near Cold Springs, Wayne County

Most Pennsylvania lakes are artificial, the result of dams built back in the thirties, forties and fifties. But as we paddled completely around the perimeter of Upper Woods Pond and found no dam, we concluded we had stumbled onto a beautiful, natural lake. Furthermore, none of the literature we had acquired on Pennsylvania lakes listed it as a reservoir. A follow-up phone call to the Fish Commission confirmed our conclusion.

Surrounded by state game lands, Upper Woods Pond is an isolated, well-kept secret. The lake is a large, irregular oval. From the launch at the northwest corner, we paddled a full circle along the entire wooded shoreline. Most striking were the clusters of bright red cardinal flowers growing at intervals around the lake. These flowers require moist soil and shade, so their needs are nicely met here.

Another burst of scarlet caught our eyes, this time high in a tree. It was a male scarlet tanager. His song, reminiscent of a robin with a sore throat, indicated he was still defending a territory.

Upper Woods Lake is isolated, pristine, and one of Pennsylvania's few public natural lakes.

Linda solos across Upper Woods Lake.

Beavers apparently like this lake as much as we do. We counted five lodges positioned around the shoreline. At the inlet of a small creek entering the lake, we found two beaver dams as well. And on the wooded hillsides surrounding the lake, fallen trees and pointy stumps indicated the colony was active.

As we paddled back to our starting point, we agreed that this was one of our favorite spots. Appearing just in time to clinch our conclusion, a small flock of hooded mergansers swam near the boat launch. As we approached, they swam away, unhurried and confident. When they reached a point about seventy-five yards into the lake, they began diving. Their serrated bill is perfect for catching minnows and other small fish.

Like wood ducks and common mergansers, hooded mergansers nest in cavities, and they are small enough to use wood duck boxes. We decided that perhaps this was a family group fledged from the large nest box we had noticed in the lake's northeast corner.

NEARBY: Lower Woods Pond, another Fish Commission lake, is just south of Upper Woods Pond. From its dam at the south end, this lake extends due north. The shoreline is wooded and irregular, with marshy fringe in some places. Don't visit this lake without stopping for a cool drink of springwater just before reaching the parking lot. A small wooden sign marks the streamside spring.

NOTE: When traveling through this area, watch for the old stone fences marking field and property lines.

GETTING THERE: From Pleasant Mount at the junction of Routes 371 and 670, proceed east on Route 371 for 4.4 miles. Turn left onto Upper Woods Road at lake sign and drive 2.4 miles. Bear to the right at fork in road and travel 0.3 mile on dirt road to launch. To get to Lower Woods Pond, continue on Route 371 another 1.5 miles past Upper Woods Road. Turn left (north) at lake sign and travel 0.3 mile. Turn left at lake sign and drive 0.25 mile to launch.

White Oak Pond
Size: 175 acres

RESTRICTIONS: nonpowered boats and electric motors only
MANAGING AGENCY: Fish and Boat Commission
LOCATION: near Aldenville, Wayne County

White Oak Pond is a refuge from the commercialism and development of the Pocono Mountain region. Local fishermen use this lake, but that's about all. And not even too many of them at one time. There are a few houses along the southern end, but these are tucked back into the trees.

Heading north from the launch, near the south-end dam, you will encounter a large "island" of mostly emergent vegetation—bur-reed, pickerelweed, cattails. Here there are many inlets to explore for waterfowl or interesting plants. The east shore near the dam features this same emergent vegetation. The lake's north end is marshy, and the west shore is wooded, as is the long arm that juts west from the dam.

Set against a backdrop of the Mosaic Mountains, White Oak Pond has its own mosaic of sedges and cattails along much of the shoreline. Great blue herons and kingfishers certainly find this a productive fishing ground. This marshy mosaic represents one of the stages of wetlands succession as open water gives way over time to forest. It evolves something like this:

A newly formed pond is at first just a body of water. Soon, however, the wind, birds, and other animals introduce zooplankton and phytoplankton such as algae.

The next stage is the growth of submerged plants such as coontail and, soon after, floating and aquatic vegetation such as water lilies and water shield. By this time, there's a rich environment for insects and invertebrates, which in turn support bird life and the fish stocked by the Fish Commission.

Along the pond's edges, water-tolerant vegetation begins to emerge—at first, herbaceous plants such as bur-reed, cattails, pickerelweed, and later, woody shrubs such as buttonbush, leatherleaf, and blueberry. This vegetation and expanding animal life attract an even greater variety of wildlife, such as muskrats, egrets, herons, red-winged blackbirds, marsh wrens, deer, raccoons, and more. Over many years these plants and animals live and die, and their remains form the sediment that slowly but surely fills in the pond. This sediment provides a rich medium for more plant growth, and the vegetation creeps farther and farther toward the center of the pond.

Eventually, water-tolerant trees appear, such as willows, sycamore, and dogwood, and the pond is well on its way to becoming a forest.

Pond gives way to marsh, and marsh gives way to forest. In human terms, it's a process that takes many decades. And there are often intervening factors: Ponds are dredged, an overpopulation of muskrats results in the elimination of marshy vegetation, fertilizers and herbicides drain into ponds . . . you get the idea.

GETTING THERE: From U.S. 6 in Waymart, east of Carbondale, take Route 296 north for 4 miles. Turn right (east) onto S.R. 4004 (White Oak Drive) at lake sign. Drive 1.5 miles to launch.

Shohola Lake

Size: 1,100 acres

RESTRICTIONS: nonpowered boats and electric motors only
MANAGING AGENCY: Game Commission
LOCATION: near Lords Valley, Pike County

From its dam at the north end, just off U.S. 6, Shohola Lake snakes and twists south, then west, then south again. There are many deeply recessed coves and inlets along the way. State game lands and Delaware State Forest surround the lake, and the lake itself is managed by the Game Commission. As we drove along the access road on the lake's heavily wooded west side, two deer crossed the road ahead of us. They paused to browse in a small, open area, oblivious to our presence.

A double rainbow greeted us the day we explored this long and narrow waterway. We didn't find a pot of gold, but we did see rich and varied wildlife populations. According to some local residents we met, Shohola Lake and Peck's Pond to the south are the best lakes in the Pocono region for spring and fall waterfowl migrations. Wood ducks and mallards represent the largest portion of waterfowl. But Lee Harshbarger, the Game Commission's Northeast Region Federal Aide Supervisor, reports that the lake's black duck population increased notably during 1993. This is significant, because black duck populations are generally declining. Their traditional northeastern bottomland habitat has been invaded during the last century by their more aggressive and adaptable western cousin, the mallard. And where mallard and black ducks overlap, they hybridize, but the mallard genes overwhelm the black duck's.

Marshy vegetation covers much of the eastern shore, and we saw lots of wood duck boxes and goose nesting platforms and an osprey platform. In fact, much of the eastern half of the lake is a designated wildlife propagation area and is off-limits to boaters. The propagation area has been extended in recent years due to nesting activity of bald eagles. With binoculars, an eagle nest can be seen in the top of a large tree almost directly across from the second boat launch. In 1992, Game Commission employees and visitors watched the nesting adults and the two chicks they raised. In 1993, the summer we visited, adult eagles were again reported at the nest, but they apparently abandoned the nest before any young were produced.

Inverted cone roofs on metal wood duck nest boxes deter predators from above. These nest boxes are a common sight on lakes throughout the state.

According to Harshbarger, Shohola Lake has a "hacking tower"— a structure where young bald eagles are released and reintroduced into an area. Over the past decade or so, some eighty eagles have been released in the area. Harshbarger explains that the Game Commission, in cooperation with Canadian wildlife officials, receives young eagles taken from nests in Saskatchewan. They are raised and fed until old enough, then released. The young birds never see who is feeding them, so they never imprint on humans. Biologists band these birds before releasing them in an effort to track their activities. Two banded pairs reportedly nested in New York, one just north of Shohola, across the state line.

If you visit Shohola in the fall, during deer season, the access road will be open the whole length of the western shore, all the way to Shohola Creek. This is a beautiful, wooded area and would make a great hike at any time of the year.

GETTING THERE: From the junction of Route 434 and U.S. 6 in north-central Pike County, travel east on U.S. 6 for two miles. Turn right at the state game lands sign (there is no lake sign). This is the lake access road. The first launch is just off the highway. A second launch is farther south, along the access road.

Migration

I hear the music before I see the players. The honking drifts down from the overcast sky. It takes a few seconds, but I find the imperfect, threadlike V. The Canada geese tell me it's October. Or March.

Whether it's spring or fall, migrating flocks of birds add a sense of wonder to any equinoctial canoe trip. Waterfowl in March, April, September, and October. Warblers and hummingbirds in May and September. Changing day length sets off the biological alarm clock that ticks in every migrant's psyche.

Bird migration is one of nature's most enduring puzzles. How can a tiny ruby-throated hummingbird, for example, find its way from Pennsylvania to the Gulf Coast and then 500 miles more across the Gulf of Mexico? Or how does a blackpoll warbler fly from Maine to South America across the open Atlantic Ocean? How does the Arctic tern make a 22,000-mile round-trip each year from Alaska to Antarctica?

And how do these birds know when to go? For that matter, why migrate at all?

The when (timing of migration) is easier to answer than the why or how. Photoperiod triggers migration. Shorter fall days and longer spring days stimulate the brain to release hormones that trigger birds to move north and south. Apparently birds possess an internal, biological clock that measures seasonal time quite precisely. It's the same kind of clock that tells trees when to shed their leaves and chipmunks when to hibernate. The standard to which biological clocks must be set is day length. Photoperiod is the only absolutely reliable natural event that signals changing environmental conditions.

Shortening days signal the approach of winter and all its problems, while lengthening days mean conditions are soon to improve. Birds respond by eating madly to acquire a layer of fat that will fuel their migratory flight. A warbler, for example, can almost double its body weight before embarking on a migratory flight.

The how of migration is even more interesting. How do migrating birds find their way?

Birds apparently possess some sort of internal map and compass mechanism that enables them to traverse unfamiliar areas and return home. So far, no one understands the internal map—how they know where they are and where they're going. But scientists have identified the internal compass.

By day, birds use landmarks and the sun, just as we would.

But birds navigate equally well on cloudy days and at night. Pigeons can even find their way when wearing frosted contact lenses that greatly reduce their vision. (Yes, researchers developed special contact lenses for birds.) They apparently possess backup compasses that take over when the primary cue (the sun) cannot be used. For example, pigeons have magnetic compounds concentrated in certain body tissues that may be sensitive to the earth's geomagnetic field. Alter the magnetic field around a pigeon's body by strapping a small magnet to its head,

and it becomes disoriented—but only on cloudy days.

Nocturnal migrants (many species migrate at night) navigate by the stars. Experiments with songbirds in planetariums have confirmed this. In the spring, for example, indigo buntings can be "tricked" into orienting to the south when shown a fall sky. The relative position between the North Star and several major constellations remains constant throughout the night, so just as photoperiod is an absolutely reliable timekeeper, certain celestial cues are absolutely reliable compasses.

That leaves the question, "Why do birds migrate?" The obvious answer is birds migrate south to escape harsh winter weather. But birds don't migrate south to escape winter so much as they migrate north to breed. Remember, most migrants spend only a few months each year in North America. They escape competition for food and nesting places in the tropics by moving north to breed. After nesting, they head back to the tropics, where food is abundant and the weather is mild. Even if resident tropical species provide stiff competition for these resources, it sure beats spending the winter in Pennsylvania.

But birds are not the only animals that migrate.

Many mammals make annual long-distance journeys in search of food. In North America tales of the ever-wandering bison herds enrich almost every account of the early wild west. And today tremendous herds of caribou roam the tundra in search of lichens. In Africa wildebeests, zebras and Thomson's gazelles follow the rains and their attendant growths of lush vegetation around the Serengeti Plain. In fact, Serengeti National Park was established to protect these herds' migration routes. If large grazing mammals that live in huge herds did not migrate, they'd run out of food in a matter of days.

Bats, like birds, may fly great distances to escape the threat of winter. In the southwest, free-tailed bats may travel 600 miles or more to south Texas or even into Mexico. In Pennsylvania, some species may travel several hundred miles to a traditional hibernaculum, while others stay put to hibernate in attics or small caves.

Even some invertebrates migrate. Atlantic lobsters move back and forth between deep water and coastal zones. In western Europe, dragonflies make conspicuous north-south trips not unlike those seen occasionally at Hawk Mountain. And biblically proportioned swarms of locusts still plague sections of northern Africa. Like the large African mammals, these grasshoppers move in response to rainfall patterns.

Perhaps the best-known invertebrate migrants are the butterflies. Many butterflies migrate, painted ladies and red admirals among them. But of the migrating butterflies, the monarch is king. Each fall these colorful orange and black insects head south for the winter. Western populations winter along the southern California coast, while monarchs east of the Rockies migrate to the Gulf Coast or central Mexico. It was only through the persistent efforts of amateur and professional entomologists that the major Mexican winter roost was discovered—a discovery that came less than fifteen years ago. It is at these winter roosts that we find the "butterfly trees"—trees so laden with sluggish, inactive monarchs that they cover every square inch of the trunk, sometimes many individuals deep.

Monarchs often migrate in large flocks. I remember one Saturday afternoon almost twenty years ago sitting in a football stadium. The game was momentarily interrupted for some fans by a band of monarchs that fluttered across the stadium from end zone to end zone. That was my introduction to migrating monarchs. Mark and recapture studies show that monarchs travel as far as 1,800 miles in just four months. They move only by day and at a leisurely pace of five to eighteen MPH.

The technique of marking butterflies is itself noteworthy. Unlike the metal bands ornithologists attach to the legs of birds to track their movements, entomologists mark monarchs by attaching tiny numbered pieces of pressure-adhesive paper to their wings.

Not only do monarchs travel great distances, they do so with unerring accuracy, just like birds. Year after year they return to the same winter areas, even the same trees. So reliable are these migratory aggregations that they have become a major tourist attraction along the southern California coast. The town of Pacific Grove, for example, proudly calls itself "Butterfly City, U.S.A."

The small forest groves in the central Mexican mountains, the final destination of many eastern monarchs, make for a much more exotic field trip. There, literally millions of monarchs congregate and wait for the cold northern winter to subside. There's little doubt that some Pennsylvania monarchs make it to Mexico each fall.

What makes the monarch migration even more amazing is that each butterfly makes this trip only once in its lifetime. Butterflies hatched in the summer migrate south in the fall and return in the spring, but die shortly after reproducing. Yet somehow each fall, inexperienced monarchs return to their ancestors' traditional wintering areas. During the winter the monarchs use very little of their fat reserves. When February rolls around, they still have plenty of stored energy for the trip north. Mating occurs before migration begins, and females lay eggs as they move northward.

Though virtually every animal group includes members that migrate, migration remains a compelling natural history mystery—one of those natural phenomena that tweaks the dreams of biologists and laymen alike.

Pecks Pond

Size: 315 acres

RESTRICTIONS: nonpowered boats and electric motors only
MANAGING AGENCY: Bureau of Forestry
LOCATION: near Dingman's Ferry, Pike County

Although Delaware State Forest surrounds Pecks Pond, there are a small community and several commercial operations along the lake's southwest edge, near the dam. But none of this detracts from the canoeing and wildlife encounters possible on this lake.

Extensive beds of water lilies lie along much of the shoreline. From the launch just east of the dam, at Peck's Pond picnic area, we headed east to explore the inlets into the sedges and pickerelweed of an extensive marsh. Canada geese, wood ducks, two great blue herons, dragonflies, and many frogs shared the evening with us.

After looking and listening for awhile, we paddled north, then due east into a long, narrow arm. In summer, when water levels are low, this area is choked with vegetation. But you can still find a canoeable channel. Later we headed north to poke around the islands large and small that dot the lake. Otters had been spotted recently on these islands, according to an employee at the local general store. "But otters come and otters go," he added.

We found a beaver lodge at the north end of the largest island. Unfortunately, we didn't see the beavers. But two other paddlers we talked to had seen several.

As we relaxed at the lakeside general store later in the day, a local man showed us photographs of area wildlife: otters, snowshoe hares, bears, coyotes, and lots of waterfowl. He told us that bald eagles come every spring to fish and feed on the lake. He and other local residents claim that Pecks Pond and nearby Shohola Lake top the list of Pocono lakes in terms of waterfowl migration.

GETTING THERE: From I-84, take Exit 8 and head south on Route 402 for 7.5 miles. Turn left at large sign for picnic area. Drive 0.6 mile to launch on left.

Promised Land Lake and Lower Lake
Size: 422 acres and 173 acres

RESTRICTIONS: nonpowered boats and electric motors only
MANAGING AGENCY: Promised Land State Park (5,808 acres)
LOCATION: near Promised Land, Pike County

Members of the Shaker religious sect who settled this area in 1878 believed it held much promise for farming and a good life. They were soon discouraged, however, by the rocky soil and eventually moved on. The name they gave the area turned out to be a cruel joke.

But for canoeists, the land that now holds two lakes and a state park is truly a "promised land." Two large lakes with complex configurations, winding channels, deeply recessed coves, islands, and miles of wooded shoreline to explore—who could ask for more? Plan to spend at least one full day exploring these two lakes. Or better yet, camp at one of the 535 wooded campsites and spend several days canoeing, wildlife watching, and hiking.

Promised Land Lake, the larger of the two lakes, is more like a series of long arms or branches than one major body of water. Imagine a large, roundish lake deeply cut by peninsulas jutting north and south and you'll have a good idea what this lake looks like. Canoeing this lake feels more like canoeing a slow, meandering river. Lower Lake is more circular, although it has wonderful coves and a long channel on the west side leading to a winding and irregular west branch.

There are four launches on Promised Land Lake and one on Lower Lake. We launched from Promised Land Lake's southern tip, at Burley Inlet, and worked our way north around Pickerel Point, south between Ridgefield Point and Conservation Island, then north again to the main beach and day use area. This is a good spot to beach for awhile and rest for the long trip back (there are food concession and rest rooms here).

On the way back we stopped at Conservation Island to hike the one-mile trail around the island. The trail, which is largely level, leads through a mature hardwood stand and provides a fairly easy walk for even young children. Occupied beaver lodges can be seen on the island's east shore, but the beavers are not usually active until evening. At one time, trail markers guided hikers and highlighted natural features, but when the markers started disappearing, the park service removed the rest. A park office employee told us that the markers will eventually be restored and maintained.

A spillway and narrow channel connect the two lakes, where water from the dam on Promised Land Lake's west side feeds into Lower Lake. It's possible to enter this channel from Lower Lake and paddle toward the dam. But we found it shallow and obstructed by beaver dams and debris when we visited in midsummer and didn't get farther than about 100 yards.

To paddle Lower Lake, we launched on the lake's northeast shore. After exploring the spillway channel and examining a large beaver lodge at the channel's mouth, we worked our way southwest.

The sun set quickly as we paddled toward Lower Lake's marshy southern shore. We'd been on the water all day, but we were willing to paddle another hour for the chance to observe an active beaver colony. Earlier in the day we'd discovered four lodges in this area. And in the spillway channel nearby, we had encountered three dams and other beaver debris. There were definitely beavers around here. Lots of them! All we had to do was wait.

As we swatted at biting flies, we saw the first ripple. Through binoculars we could see the characteristic ears, the eyes just above the water, and the top of the back barely visible. It was a beaver, all right. Then it submerged, leaving behind a trail of bubbles.

We were picking our way through the lily pads when we saw another beaver. This one dove toward a lodge and disappeared. A third hugged the shoreline and disappeared around a bend. We spotted two more swimming and diving in the middle of the lake. It was a five-beaver night!

We found interesting plant life that evening as well, including the tiny flowers of two different bladderwort species. These submerged plants send flower stalks above the water to bloom. We saw both purple and yellow flowers.

First open to the public in 1905, Promised Land State Park is one of Pennsylvania's oldest state parks. Many park facilities used today were built by the Civilian Conservation Corps in the 1930s. The park features more than thirty miles of hiking trails, year-round camping facilities, twelve rustic rental cabins, boat rentals, and three swimming beaches. For more information, call the park office at 717-676-3428.

NEARBY: Promised Land State Park is surrounded by Delaware State Forest. Also close by is the 2,765-acre Bruce Lake Natural Area. Bruce Lake is a natural 48-acre glacial lake. Both it and the nearby 60-acre

Egypt Meadow Lake can be canoed, but only after a long portage (2.5 and 0.5 miles, respectively). The area is only open to foot traffic. Also nearby is Lake Wallenpaupack, a 5,700-acre lake open to unrestricted motorboating.

GETTING THERE: From I-84, take Exit 7 (Promised Land State Park) and head south on Route 390 for five miles to the park office.

Southeast Region

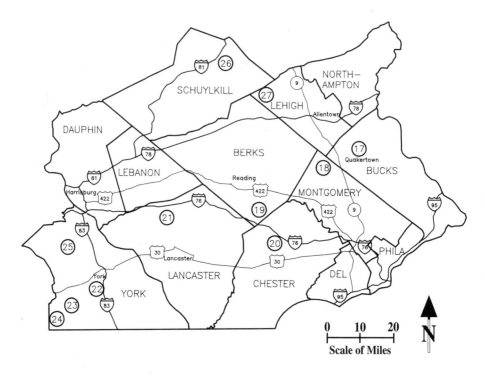

17. Lake Nockamixon
18. Green Lane Reservoir
19. Hopewell Lake and Scotts Run Lake
20. Marsh Creek Lake
21. Speedwell Forge Lake
22. Lake Redman and Lake Williams
23. Lake Marburg
24. L.B. Sheppard Reservoir
25. Pinchot Lake
26. Tuscarora Lake
27. Leaser Lake

Southeast Pennsylvania is the most densely populated part of the state. The lakes here generally see heavy use and are often surrounded by extensive residential areas or development. We both grew up here in the southeast, and every time we come back for a visit, we're dismayed to see even more development. But there are still large tracts of land set aside as state and county parks or game lands. Many of these feature beautiful man-made lakes and reservoirs that sustain wildlife and humans alike.

Historical sites and buildings abound in the southeast. Colonial-style stone farmhouses 200 to 250 years old are common here. Philadelphia, Valley Forge, Hopewell Furnace, Daniel Boone's homestead, and many more important sites are found in this region. Search out these sites and take time to appreciate the historic architecture and countryside as you visit this area's lakes and reservoirs.

The southeast, particulary Lancaster County, is also "Amish Country." Rolling hills and well-manicured fields, farmhouses, and barns characterize this well-known area. During the summer, stop by the many Amish fruit and vegetable stands to sample the area's bounty.

Harrisburg, the state capital, is found in the southeast, as well as the "Chocolatetown" of Hershey, where street lamps are shaped like Hershey Kisses.

The Susquehanna River flows along the region's western edge. The river and its tributaries offer many excellent paddling adventures. But don't let the river's "quiet" appearance fool you. Just the sheer quantity of water flowing through this system produces a tremendously strong current and can offer a formidable challenge to even experienced canoeists.

Another unique canoeing experience can be had on Darby Creek in the John Heinz National Wildlife Refuge at Tinicum, located just one mile north of Philadelphia International Airport. Waterfowl and wading birds are common here, but a good bird to look and listen for during the nesting season is the marsh wren. We mention Tinicum for two reasons: one, to illustrate that even in the most urban setting, quality canoeing experiences are possible; and two, this "creek" is so sluggish that it certainly qualifies as "quiet."

Lake Nockamixon

Size: 1,450 acres

RESTRICTIONS: 10 HP limit
MANAGING AGENCY: Nockamixon State Park (5,283 acres)
LOCATION: near Quakertown, Bucks County

Seven miles long, with twenty-seven miles of shoreline, Lake Nockamixon is a beautiful, undeveloped lake that serves the metropolitan areas of Philadelphia, Allentown, Quakertown, Bethlehem, and Easton. The horsepower limit for motorboats keeps the crowds small. We spent an early summer weekday there and saw very few other boats. And since most of the shoreline is wooded and irregular, with coves to explore along the lake's entire length, it's easy to avoid other people.

From the Tohickon Creek dam at the lake's extreme eastern edge, the lake branches into two directions. The main body of the lake curves slightly northwest, then southwest, ending about seven miles away in a two-pronged fork. A much smaller branch extends almost three miles due north from the dam. According to local anglers, the lake offers excellent striped bass and walleye fishing.

Fingers extending from the lake's southern- and northernmost reaches promise the most excitement for the quiet water canoeist. At these spots, the vegetation becomes more marshy, and there is a greater chance for encountering wildlife. Also, the fingers extend under Route 563 bridges at both ends of the lake, which adds to the adventure. Two launch sites serve these finger areas—Haycock access at the north end and Three Mile Run access at the south end.

We put in at Haycock, headed northeast, and paddled under the Route 563 bridge into the finger that extends west. The shoreline along here features stands of conifers mixed with the more dominant deciduous trees and marshy vegetation lining the perimeter. We found a colony of cliff swallows nesting under the bridge. In the coves along the way we saw kingfishers and green-backed herons. You can also head east from the launch site and paddle toward the dam. Along the way, look for two lovely coves to explore on the north shore.

At Three Mile Run access to the south, we headed for the other Route 563 bridge and a finger of the lake that juts west. Again the wooded shoreline features patches of conifers. Closer to the bridge there are white water lilies, smartweed, and pickerelweed.

Just before the bridge, a cove opens on the north shore. The narrow mouth of the cove leads into what looks and feels like a nice-sized pond. The cove fills a basinlike area, where shrubs, small trees, and herbaceous plants cover the surrounding hillsides. These hillsides are in an early successional stage from meadow or grassland to woods. We drifted lazily for awhile here, birding and enjoying the cove's privacy.

We saw kingfishers diving from trees on a rocky outcrop near the bridge and lots of sleeping mallards, perching green-backed herons, basking turtles, and leaping bass. At the bridge, the finger really narrows and becomes rocky and impassable. Hardier canoeists could portage twenty or thirty yards past these rocks to reach the shallow upper reaches of the finger and its extension to Tohickon Creek. This area has a marshier feel to it.

Canoes and other boats can be rented at the marina. The park features a swimming pool (swimming is not permitted in the lake), bicycle and horse trails, ample picnicking areas, a youth hostel, and family cabins. Several private campgrounds are located nearby.

For more information call the park office at 215-538-2151. For information on local accommodations and camping, call the Bucks County Tourist Commission at 215-345-4552 or 800-836-BUCKS. The Weisel Youth Hostel can be reached at 215-536-8749.

NEARBY: If you enjoy environmental education, visit the nature center at nearby Peace Valley Park. The entrance for the nature center is along New Galina Road, just a mile south of Route 313 on the north shore of Lake Galina. The center features exhibits of the local flora and fauna and a gift shop stocked with unique items for nature lovers. Look for the large colony of barn swallows nesting in the nearby barn. And stroll past the parking lot on a short path leading to a bridge over the northeast tip of the lake. Here, the lake ends in a marshy area designated as wildlife sanctuary. The footbridge affords the only close look at this area and its abundant wildlife (swans, Canada geese, ducks, herons, waders and shorebirds, turtles). The 360-acre lake itself is canoeable, but it's basically a large, open oval with mostly mowed shoreline. Spring and fall waterfowl migrations are notable, but the birds could be viewed as easily from shore. Also, there is a twenty-dollar county launch fee for private boat access. Canoes and rowboats can be rented.

GETTING THERE: Lake Nockamixon lies 5 miles east of Quakertown and 9 miles west of Doylestown, just off Route 313. From

Quakertown, travel east 5 miles on Route 313 from the junction of 663 and 309 (663 becomes 313). Turn left onto Route 563 and go 3.6 miles to the park entrance and main office. This is the entrance to the marina and boat rental concession. To get to the Haycock access, travel another 3.4 miles north of the main office on 563. (Watch for the designated wildflower areas all along this part of 563.)

You can also reach the Haycock launch site from the northwest and Route 611. Exit 611 on Route 412 and head north for 0.5 mile. Turn left (south) onto Route 563 and drive 0.9 mile to Haycock access or 4.3 miles to park office.

From the southwest, take Route 611 to Route 313, head west on 313 about 10 miles to Route 563. Turn right and proceed 3.6 miles to park office or 9 miles to Haycock access.

The second access we recommend is Three Mile Run. This is located at the lake's southwest end. Three Mile Run Road is 0.7 mile from the Routes 313 and 563 intersection. Turn north and drive 1 mile to access area on the left.

Bullfrogs

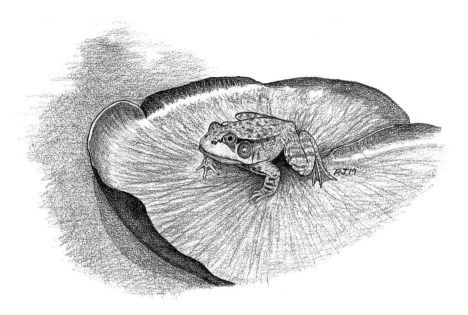

The crimson sky faded in the west. On the other side of the lake moonshine illuminated the marsh where we sat quietly in our canoe. The evening symphony of natural sounds had begun about an hour earlier. The trills of myriad insects filled the air, a night heron croaked, and a great horned owl hooted in the distance. A beaver surfaced next to the canoe, saw us, and immediately slapped its tail and submerged in indignation. Then, from the cattails just twenty yards away, "Jug-o'-rummm!" "Jug-o'-rummm!" The booming bass echoed across the marsh. It was June. Time for bullfrogs to take center stage.

Along the edges of marshes, ponds, and lakes, similar scenarios unfold every night. The hour before and after sunset can be as rewarding for a quiet water paddler as a trip at sunrise because most wildlife is crepuscular—most active at dawn and dusk.

Bullfrogs are the last frogs to breed each spring. Spring peepers and wood frogs begin singing and breeding in March. Other frogs and toads gear their activities to early and midspring.

Bullfrogs, on the other hand, emerge in early spring but delay breeding until late May. Their basso profundo announces the onset of summer. Any quiet body of water surrounded with dense vegetation is likely to shelter bullfrogs—for example, lakes ringed with cattails, water lilies, or sedges.

Both sexes of bullfrogs vocalize, but the "jug-o'-rum" mating song of the male is the loudest and best known. Other calls signal territory ownership, warning, and distress. Bullfrog distress calls can be so long and loud that a turn-of-the-century biologist wrote, "We hasten to release the frog, for fear our neighbors will accuse us of cruelty to children."

Bullfrogs begin breeding in late spring and continue well into summer. Males sing (or perhaps "bellow" is a better description) to attract females to their territory. Each male sings from a station along the bank that he returns to night after night. Mating occurs in the water. A male mounts a female and grips her tightly with his forelimbs. Herpetologists call the embrace amplexus. As the female releases a stream of eggs, the male fertilizes them. Each female lays 1,000 to as many as 25,000 eggs on the surface of the water around pieces of aquatic vegetation. The eggs hatch in three to five days. Double broods are common. After a spring spawning in late May or early June, bullfrogs repeat the process in late July.

Bullfrog tadpoles grow slowly, reaching a length of one inch by the end of their first summer. Before transforming into adults, however, they grow extraordinarily large. Bullfrog tadpoles often reach lengths of six inches or more before metamorphosis. They require several years to reach reproductive age. The tadpole stage lasts one or two years. Young bullfrogs then need another two years to reach sexual maturity. This means bullfrogs are often four years old before they breed.

Like most frogs, which eat insects, spiders, and earthworms, bullfrogs are also voracious predators. They attack any live animal smaller than themselves—no mean feat for a frog that may measure eight inches from nose to butt. A sit-and-wait style rewards patient bullfrogs. They sit motionless for long stretches of time, yet remain alert to any movement. If danger threatens, such as a canoe drifting too close, it's hop, splash, and off to deep water. But if a crayfish, minnow, or dragonfly ventures near, it's mealtime.

But bullfrogs don't limit themselves to small prey. A few years ago a student of mine found small turtles in the stomachs of several large bullfrogs. Other biologists have found mice, birds, ducklings, smaller frogs (including smaller bullfrogs), and even hatchling alligators in bullfrog stomachs!

Despite their predatory nature, bullfrogs do not sit at the top of the food chain. A variety of aquatic predators make meals of bullfrogs: muskies, pike, herons, raccoons, bobcats, mink, otters, and even owls are just some of the larger predators that eat bullfrogs.

On this evening, though, the bullfrogs' attention was not focused on eating or being eaten. This night they were preoccupied with sex. "Jug-o'-rummm! Jug-o'-rummm!"

Green Lane Reservoir

Size: 805 acres

RESTRICTIONS: nonpowered boats and electric motors only
MANAGING AGENCY: Green Lane Reservoir Park (2,491 acres)
LOCATION: near Green Lane, Montgomery County

Green Lane Reservoir ranks high on our list of canoeing and birding hot spots. Along its nineteen miles of irregularly configured shoreline, the lake hosts more than 260 species of birds, including shorebirds, waterfowl, waders, bald eagles, and songbirds. From its dam in the small village of Green Lane, the reservoir snakes northward about 4.5 miles, wandering into numerous coves, inlets, and fingers along the way. On the vast acreage of the lake and park, you can forget for awhile the new housing developments sprouting up all around here. This once-rural area where we both grew up is really just suburban Philadelphia now. In fact, the reservoir is owned by Philadelphia Suburban Water Company, which yielded recreational easement rights to the county in 1983.

Only one launch serves privately owned boats—the Walt Road access at the north end. From here, you can head northwest toward the Route 663 bridge and the wildlife sanctuary. The sanctuary is off-limits to boats, but you can see many shorebirds and waders in the mudflats from near the bridge. And bald eagles are frequently spotted. Seasonal fluctuations in water level here affect canoeability, of course.

If you have the whole day and are feeling strong, you can work your way southward toward the dam, exploring coves as you go. Be sure to take a lake map along. And don't forget to save some energy for the return trip.

Spring migration, from mid-April through early June, would be a great time to visit the reservoir. During this time you could expect to see such species as common loons, double-crested cormorants, great egrets, herons, all types of ducks, osprey, bald eagles, plovers, yellowlegs, sandpipers, terns, Virginia rails, red-headed woodpeckers, purple martins, and more. Local birders take their reservoir birding seriously. They keep a daily log of bird sightings at the nature center. Ask for the reservoir bird list, available in neatly printed booklet form. Also available is a flora guide.

Hiking and horse trails crisscross the park, following the shoreline in some spots. No camping is allowed, but the park office can provide information about nearby campsites. A boat rental concession operates on the west shore at the south end, near the park office.

Now the down side: For nonresidents of Montgomery County, a forty-dollar fee is charged to launch private boats. (If you have family members living in Montgomery County and they go boating with you, the fee is waived.) This fee covers launch privileges for an entire year but is charged even if you only spend one day there. This seems steep, but given the area's tremendous resources and wildlife diversity, we decided it was worth it. Canoeists who live in surrounding counties could easily make this fee pay off.

Also, in 1993 a zebra mussel quarantine was in effect. All boats had to sit on the premises in dry dock for ten days before entering the water.

NEARBY: Don't miss the chance to visit the park's nature center, located off Route 29 just north of the dam and Green Lane. In late spring and summer, look for the center's butterfly garden. Such "weedy" favorites as bee balm, butterfly milkweed, coneflower, zinnias, and trumpet creeper bloom in profusion, attracting a variety of butterflies.

GETTING THERE: From Route 663 just south of East Greenville, turn east onto Montgomery Avenue. Go 0.8 mile, then turn right at the crossroad (at a high school) onto Walt Road. Drive 0.5 mile to launch. Or from Red Hill, on Route 29, turn south onto 11th Street at sign for boat launch. Several blocks south, at the high school, 11th Street becomes Walt Road. Drive 0.5 mile to launch.

Hopewell and Scotts Run Lakes
Size: 68 and 21 acres

RESTRICTIONS: nonpowered boats and electric motors only
MANAGING AGENCY: French Creek State Park (7,339 acres)
LOCATION: near Geigertown, Berks County

Canoeists visiting French Creek State Park get "two for one." Hopewell Lake and the smaller Scotts Run Lake, both located within park boundaries, combine to provide a fun, easy day of quiet water canoeing.

Hopewell Lake, named for the nearby historic iron furnace village, was created in the early 1800s to power the furnace's blast machinery. From its dam at the east end, water was channeled one-quarter mile to a giant waterwheel that powered the furnace bellows. Today, the popular and heavily used area proves that even a developed lake contains natural treasures just waiting to be discovered.

From the launch at the southwest end, we headed east, intending to explore the lake's entire perimeter. Just east of the boat rental dock and swimming pool on the south shore we noticed a Louisiana waterthrush bobbing at water's edge. We drifted to within ten feet of it. Amazingly, the bird did not fly off, and we had many minutes to observe carefully. We didn't even need binoculars to see its characteristic white eye-line, rusty brown back, pink legs, salmon-colored flank patch, and white belly with dark spots. Louisiana waterthrushes are uncommon, so it was an exciting find. These birds live and nest on the ground, usually along rivers, streams, or wooded swamps. They walk, instead of hopping like most birds, bobbing their tails constantly. They work the water's edge, probing for aquatic insects, spiders, and other invertebrates. You have a much better chance of seeing one from your canoe than approaching by land.

In a large, northeast cove, near the dam, we found clusters of sunfish nests. The nests consist of "cups" of clean gravel, eighteen to twenty-four inches across. The female sunfish builds the nest by fanning the area with its fins to wash away silt and debris. These fish can even remove pond weeds to clear an area. After laying eggs in the nest, the female continues to fan it to keep the eggs free of silt and debris, thus keeping them well oxygenated. We counted dozens and dozens of sunfish nests at this end of the lake.

We continued our counterclockwise shoreline exploration, entering a large marshy area in the northwest corner. This is where Scotts Run enters the lake. We followed Scotts Run a short way upstream, enjoying the cool shade and dark woods.

Another cove juts southwest, just south of the launch. Here we found ourselves among dozens of mallards and Canada geese in shallow, soiled waters. This waterfowl hangout is best left to the waterfowl.

Much smaller Scotts Run Lake is basically rectangular in shape. It's popular with trout fishermen, but it's also a pleasant canoe outing. The area could easily become crowded, however, so plan to arrive early in the morning or visit in the early spring or fall. Trout season begins in mid-April, and Scotts Run Lake is heavily stocked with brook and rainbow trout.

Behind the dam, which is located in the southeast corner, we found a nest box and a whole family of young bluebirds. The mowed dam breast provided perfect habitat for hunting insects and grubs. Birds were also abundant along the wooded shoreline. We saw a scarlet tanager, veery, wood thrush, red-eyed vireo, and robins. On the water, a small flock of molting male mallards dodged our canoe and hurried toward the marshy northwest corner. Molting waterfowl cannot fly and are extremely vulnerable for four to eight weeks, depending on the species. They tend to seek safety in numbers during the molt.

The park has 260 year-round camping sites (most with access to showers and flush toilets) and modern furnished cabins. There are more than thirty-two miles of hiking trails, including a TRIM Orienteering self-guided course. A TRIM course is a permanently marked course, as opposed to the portable markers used in competitions. The course at French Creek allows participants to find orange and white markers in the woods by using a map and compass. The course features a small circle (orienteering trails are laid out in circles) for those with just a casual interest or a larger circle for the more ambitious. Simply go to the park office and ask for a map and instructions. It's an activity enjoyed by all ages. The Delaware Valley Orienteering Association sponsors various competitions (some national) at French Creek and other state parks. Some of the group's members even practice canoe orienteering, although that activity is not yet conducted on an organized level. If you visit nearby Hopewell Village, look at the bookshop display of three large colored orienteering maps produced by the Delaware Valley Orienteering Association. These maps, which include individual rocks and even depressions in the earth, will give you an idea of the maps used in this fascinating sport. For information about the French Creek course or orienteering in general, contact Ed and Judy Scott at 610-582-2128.

For more information, call the park office at 215-582-1514.

NEARBY: Top off your canoeing experience at French Creek State Park with a visit to Hopewell Furnace National Historic Site, just a mile past Park Road on Route 345. This iron furnace supplied many of the cannons, tools, and weapons used in the revolutionary war. You can tour the re-created village and furnace and see actual demonstrations of iron making. An air-conditioned visitor's center provides informative exhibits and slide shows. In one good day you can easily canoe both lakes and still enjoy several hours at Hopewell Furnace.

GETTING THERE: From Route 100 south of Pottstown, turn west onto Route 23 for 3.6 miles to St. Peter's Road. (There's a sign for St. Peter's Village.) Turn right (north) and go 1.5 miles (passing the village) to a stop sign. Turn left onto Harmonyville Road (S.R. 4018). Go just 0.2 mile and bear right onto Hopewell Road (S.R. 4020, later on called Baptism Road). Go 2.2 miles to stop sign and intersection with Route 345. This is the entrance to Hopewell Furnace National Historic Site. Turn left and proceed south on Route 345 for a little over a mile to the sign for the park entrance. Turn right on Park Road. The park office is just ahead on the right. Hopewell Lake is just past the office. To get to Scotts Run Lake, continue on Park Road 0.7 mile past Hopewell Lake. Turn left at lake sign, go 0.5 mile, and turn left again to launch.

This is a very scenic drive through an old, colonial part of Berks County.

Marsh Creek Lake

Size: 535 acres

RESTRICTIONS: nonpowered boats and electric motors only
MANAGING AGENCY: Marsh Creek State Park (1,705 acres)
LOCATION: near Eagle, Chester County

Nestled in the rolling hills of Marsh Creek State Park, beautiful Marsh Creek Lake helps visitors forget for a little while the suburban sprawl surrounding them. From the dam, the main body of the lake extends north. Two long arms and one shorter one branch off to the east. At its northwestern corner, a fourth arm extends north, then northeast for well over a mile. You could easily spend a day here, exploring miles of shoreline and various inlets and coves. Or you could enjoy one portion of the lake in just several hours.

Windy conditions produce choppy waters in the main portion of the lake. This is where sailing is popular. Most canoeists and kayakers prefer to hug the shorelines and avoid open waters.

There are two boat launch sites, both in the middle of the lake and directly across from each other, but separated by many road miles due to the lake's sprawling configuration. The main launch site is located on the east shore, near the office, the boat rental concession, and the swimming pool. Always looking to avoid the crowds, we used the west launch site. (This launch offers twenty-four-hour fishing and boating access.)

According to park employees, Marsh Creek Lake is the birding hot spot of Chester County. Birders here report loons, ospreys, whistling swans, bald eagles, egrets, herons, and, of course, many ducks and geese. On a hot summer day, we saw green-backed herons, two broods of wood ducks, and a mallard family.

But our attention was focused more on wildlife under the surface. We found the clear water excellent for fish watching. Floating from the west launch site northward along the shoreline, we could easily see at least six feet below the surface. We watched sunfish and bass as they moved silently among the submerged vegetation. A fourteen-inch bass emerged from an underwater tree stump as we floated by. We also saw many sunfish nests among the sometimes gravelly, sometimes weedy bottoms.

Camping is not permitted within the park, but a private campground on Route 282 is only a mile away. There is a youth hostel facility within the park. For information, call the park office at 215-458-8515.

GETTING THERE: From the Pennsylvania Turnpike, take Exit 23 (Downingtown) and head north on Route 100 for 1.5 miles. Turn left onto Park Road, in the small village of Eagle (there's a small sign for the park). Proceed 1.9 miles to park entrance and east launch site. To get to the west launch site, from Route 100, take Park Road 0.1 mile to Little Conestoga Road. Turn right (north) and go 2.6 miles to Styer Road. Bear left. (Styer Road becomes Marshall Road.) Travel 1.2 miles to stop sign. Turn left on Route 282 and go 1.1 miles to Lyndell Road. Turn left (there's a sign for the park) and proceed 1.2 miles to launch site access road on left. This is also where the youth hostel and horse stables are located.

The west shore launch site is open twenty-four hours for fishing and boating. The rest of the park opens at 8:00 A.M. and closes at sunset.

Speedwell Forge Lake
Size: 106 acres

RESTRICTIONS: nonpowered boats and electric motors only
MANAGING AGENCY: Fish and Boat Commission
LOCATION: near Lititz, Lancaster County

Some of our best wildlife encounters occurred on small Fish Commission lakes just off the beaten path. Such was the case at Speedwell Forge Lake. Due north of Lancaster, this lake lies amidst farm fields and rural residential areas. But enough of the shoreline is wooded to provide wildlife shelter and nesting areas and give canoeists a feeling of isolation.

From its east-end dam, the lake reaches west, curves north, then curves west again. Canoeists can choose between two launches, one on either side of the Brubaker Valley Road bridge. We launched from the north side of the bridge, off Lakeview Road. A large flock of Canada geese "launched" with us. We followed close behind, managing to glide by for a good look and a little race. The geese were molting. We could see the absence of primary feathers when they flapped their wings and "ran" along the water.

We headed east toward a cove just north of the bridge. A great blue heron fished at the end of the cove. Later we paddled under the bridge and south for awhile, observing purple martins flying overhead.

Flocks of Canada geese, such as these on Speedwell Forge Lake, are found on virtually every lake in Pennsylvania.

Soon we headed back north toward the mudflats at the lake's northern tip. The geese apparently had the same idea, and we raced most of the way. Halfway there, a black-crowned night heron flew overhead and landed on a log barely above water level. As their name suggests, these herons feed and move around mostly at night. It was unusual to see one in broad daylight. We stopped paddling and took a good, long look. We could easily see its black crown and back and white neck and belly. It just crouched on its log, staring at us. We moved on.

As we approached the mudflats, the water became very shallow—barely five inches deep in some spots. But we found the channel where Hammer Creek flows into the lake. Along this channel we saw a spotted sandpiper bobbing and probing the mud on a small, marshy island. Two killdeer worked the sandbar nearby. A family of mallards dodged among young willows sprouting in the shallows.

Paddling back to the launch, we were surprised to see the night heron still perched right where we had left it. As we approached, a green-backed heron landed near the black-crowned. Seconds later, they both took off, allowing us to compare their size. The black-crowned was much larger and stockier, with a considerably longer wingspan. It flew toward the south end of the lake, croaking its deep, guttural "wok, wok" as it flew.

There is a picnic pavilion at the launch north of Brubaker Valley Road and a comfort station at the other launch, just 0.2 mile south.

GETTING THERE: From U.S. 30 in Lancaster, drive north on Route 501 for 10.4 miles. Turn left (west) onto Brubaker Valley Road and proceed 1 mile to the bridge, which bisects the lake. Turn left to launch by the bridge, or turn right onto Lakeview Road just past the bridge, and go 0.2 mile to a second launch. (One mile before Brubaker Valley Road is a sign for the lake, on Zartman Mill Road. This is the long way to the launch. Ignore the sign and proceed to Brubaker Valley.)

Route 501 between Lancaster and I-78 passes historic and scenic countryside, including the town of Lititz, founded in 1756, and rolling Amish farmlands, where Amish farmers work their fields with teams of horses. To the north, foothills rise on the horizon, the first evidence of central Pennsylvania's mountainous region. On the highway, be careful of horses and buggies.

Lake Redman and Lake Williams
Size: 290 and 220 acres

RESTRICTIONS: nonpowered boats and electric motors only
MANAGING AGENCY: William H. Kain County Park (1,675 acres)
LOCATION: near Jacobus, York County

Owned by York Water Company, Lake Redman and Lake Williams provide water for a large urban population. But they also serve as recreational areas leased and maintained by York County.

From its dam just east of George Street, Lake Redman curves southeast for more than a mile, then hooks northeast under I-83 before continuing southeast again into a long, narrow marshy area. I-83 parallels a large portion of the east shore, and highway noise seriously detracts from the quiet water experience. But when the lake passes under the interstate, it twists away from the noise.

We launched just west of the interstate bridge, then paddled under the bridge and the Church Street bridge as we followed the lake south. Woods surround this southern tip. Two kingfishers and a great blue heron fished the shallows, while a fair number of anglers worked the banks. Judging from the tangles of monofilament line we found, this appears to be a popular fishing spot.

Lake Redman is also a popular canoeing spot. A rental concession rents canoes, rowboats, and paddleboats adjacent to the public launch, and it appeared to be doing a brisk business the morning we visited.

We much preferred Lake Williams. This W-shaped lake features steeply wooded shoreline and much more solitude than Lake Redman. Only privately owned boats use this lake, and those must be carried in on top of a car. There is no launching ramp, only a small wooden dock near the parking lot.

From the launch you can head west toward the dam, which is located at the beginning of the W (top left corner). There's a neat little cove just north of the dam, where the clear water showcases sunfish and small bass. We had fun fish watching here.

A subsurface algae bloom colored the water deep green during our early July visit. That, and the reflection of its wooded slopes, gives Lake Williams a dark, haunting appearance. We loved it. And dark as it appeared, the water was so clear that we did more fish watching than bird watching.

South George Street runs right between the two lakes. If you get a chance, pull over here and check out the Lake Redman spillway. We saw three yellowlegs (a large shorebird) and lots of killdeer in the water here and many barn swallows and rough-winged swallows under the South George Street Bridge. The spillway passes under the bridge, where water from Lake Redman enters Lake Williams along its marshy, northeast shore.

NEARBY: The Susquehanna River borders York County and provides countless canoeing and boating opportunities. Some people think that the Susquehanna, with its reputation as a river that's "a mile wide and a foot deep," really ranks as quiet water. But that's not true. This river has a strong current. And as river-canoeing experts such as Roger Healy can tell you, just the sheer volume of water passing through this system creates many potentially dangerous situations. Once, when Healy and a fellow canoeist caught their canoe on a submerged rock and tipped, they had to float two miles downstream before they could drag their canoe to the bank.

Healy, who knows the lower Susquehanna like the back of his hand, and his wife, Amelia, own a bed-and-breakfast (The 1854 House) in Wrightsville, just northeast of York and along the river. In addition to the Susquehanna, Healy regularly canoes Muddy, Otter, and Codorus creeks, all of which drain into the Susquehanna. Most of all, he loves to talk about canoeing hot spots and where the best put-ins are. He even offered to show us some of his favorite routes. If you're in the area and need nighttime accommodations, we highly recommend The 1854 House and its canoeing enthusiast owners. For information, call the Healys at 717-252-4643.

TIP: Be sure to try Maryland crabs while you're in the area. York County has many wonderful seafood restaurants.

GETTING THERE: From I-83 south of York, take Exit 4 and head west on Route 182 for 0.4 mile to George Street at the stoplight. Turn left at park sign onto South George Street and travel 2 miles to Church Street. Turn left (there's another park sign) and drive 0.6 mile to parking lot and launch on Lake Redman. To get to Lake Williams, continue south on George Sreet for 0.1 mile past Church Street and turn right onto Water Street. Drive 0.4 mile to launch.

NOTE: Only cartop boats are permitted at Lake Williams. There is no launch ramp for trailers.

Lake Marburg
Size: 1,275 acres

RESTRICTIONS: 10 H.P. limit
MANAGING AGENCY: Codorus State Park (3,320 acres)
LOCATION: near Hanover, York County

Named for the town it now covers, Lake Marburg was created in 1966 when Codorus Creek was dammed by the P.H. Glatfelter Paper Company. The company needed water for its operations, and the commonwealth saw the recreational potential of such an impoundment. From its dam, built and still owned by the paper company, the lake stretches about 3.5 miles southwest. One long arm branches off to the southeast then forks, with one prong continuing southeast and the other heading due south. Numerous other coves and fingers combine to give the lake twenty-six fascinating miles of shoreline. The urge to explore hits hard. Unfortunately, motorboats up to 10 H.P. may use the lake, sometimes detracting from the solitude and wildlife that canoeists would like to find. Sailing is also popular, particularly along the northeast half. Avoid the developed east shore and you'll be okay.

Of eight launch sites, we'd recommend two for canoes.

The first is the Black Rock bridge launch at the lake's southwest edge. This small launch allows easy access to two areas rich in wildlife—Black Rock Flats, at the headwaters of Codorus Creek (West Branch) and a marshy area west of the launch where Furnace Creek enters the lake.

We put in at Black Rock and headed due west toward the Furnace Creek headwaters. Paddling under Black Rock bridge we counted six globular cliff swallow nests (with birds inside), a phoebe nest, and an active rock dove (pigeon) nest. There wasn't much clearance between our heads and the bridge, so we got a really close look at these nests.

Past the bridge, we worked our way past some mudflats to Furnace Creek on the marsh's south side. (The channel is easy to find but may be impassable during dry times of the year.) A family of green-backed herons greeted us at the mouth of the creek. Unlike many herons and egrets, green-backs don't nest in colonies away from water. They nest individually, near the same water they fish. We counted at least seven perched on low branches or logs. It was an incredible sight, and loud, squawking "kyowk" sounds soon filled the air as they flushed at our approach. Following the creek a short distance, we encountered several molting mallards. Late in summer, when low water levels expose the mudflats, you could expect to find shorebirds probing in the mud.

Next we explored Black Rock Flats, a marshy cove that juts south of the launch. A wood duck flushed from its cover in the sedges. A great blue heron fished from an exposed log. And everywhere, painted turtles popped out of the water to check us out.

It was here that we first encountered a natural phenomenon that would mystify us for weeks. Later we would encounter it at lakes all over the state. In the shallow waters of the cove's marshy tip we noticed several large, clear blobs attached to submerged sticks or stumps. The large gelatinous masses were as large as footballs.

Our first impression was that it was an amphibian egg mass of some sort, but when we examined it in hand, we could see no embryos. Scott sliced one open with a knife and discovered that the inside consisted of clear Jell-O-like material. The outer surface was covered with small textured plates. Scott suspected it was an invertebrate of some sort, but it had been many years since that course in invertebrate zoology.

The next time we returned home we checked our reference books and called some colleagues. We concluded the organism was *Pectinella magnifica,* a common and widespread freshwater bryozoan. The textured plates on the surface of the blob were the individuals making up the massive colony. Individuals eat tiny planktonic organisms that they catch with a set of small tentacles called the lophophore. Bryozoans are a major, but rather obscure, group of invertebrates studied by a few widely scattered specialists. This creature has no doubt puzzled curious boaters and anglers for years.

At the end of the steeply wooded cove we found Codorus Creek after only one false start. It's amazing how the eyes can play tricks when you are trying to find a channel through marshy vegetation. We explored the creek a few hundred yards until it became too narrow and clogged with streamside vegetation.

The second launch we'd recommend is Mooring Cove on the west shore, near the lake's northeast end. From here, you can head southeast to explore Long Island and Round Island. These good-sized islands are the only two on the lake. Past Long Island, you can paddle southeast toward Third Bridge and Marburg Flats, more than 1.5 miles away. Or veer southward toward Wildasin Flats, past Second Bridge.

Two different boat rental concessions are located on the east shore. A 198-site park campground is open from mid-April to mid-October.

And check out the purple martin colonies at picnic area M-2, overlooking the Marina.

For more information, call the park office at 717-637-2816.

NEARBY: Historic Gettysburg National Military Park is about fifteen miles west of Lake Marburg on Route 30.

GETTING THERE: From Hanover, at the junction of Route 94 and Route 116, head east on Route 116 for 1.5 miles, then turn right on Route 216 and travel east 2.2 miles to park office and First Bridge. Route 216 continues east through the park, crossing the lake two more times at Second Bridge and Third Bridge. *Or* from I-83 south of Loganville, take Exit 2 and head west on Route 216 for 15.9 miles to Third Bridge and the turnoff for the main launch area. Continue west on Route 216 through the park to the park office and launches on the west shore.

To get to the Black Rock Bridge access, drive 1 mile north of the park office on Route 216, then turn left onto Bankert Road and drive 1.7 miles. Turn left at the stop sign onto Black Rock Road and go 0.5 mile to access on left. To get to the Mooring Cove access, take Smith Station Road, just east of the park office, for less than 2 miles, then turn right onto Hoff Road and go 1.5 miles to access.

Lake Marburg is a large, potentially confusing area. Make sure to pick up a map at the park office before you begin your explorations. If you arrive when the office is closed, there is a large map displayed just outside the office. This will at least help you orient.

L.B. Sheppard Reservoir (Long Arm Dam)
Size: 240 acres

RESTRICTIONS: nonpowered boats and electric motors only
MANAGING AGENCY: Fish and Boat Commission
LOCATION: near Hanover, York County

You just never know what you're going to find while quiet water canoeing. There we were, paddling along the northern end of Sheppard Reservoir on a late afternoon in early July, when we spotted a single common loon swimming toward us less than 100 yards away. It was the flash of white on its chest that first caught our attention. A closer look through the binoculars revealed the unexpected find: a bird with a large, black, thick bill and dark head sitting low in the water. It was a profile we recognized. But we couldn't believe we were seeing a loon this far south in midsummer.

Loons nest in northern New York, New England, and Canada. Yet here we were in southern York County, almost on the Maryland border. We froze, binoculars glued to our eyes, studying the bird as it leisurely swam toward the west shore. There it was—the telltale black-and-white-striped back. Definitely a loon! Perhaps it was injured, we speculated. Or perhaps it had lost its mate and was heading south early. Either way, after our initial euphoria, we felt a little saddened at the sight of this lonely loon.

Sheppard Reservoir is a must-see! You can easily spend half a day or more exploring its irregular and fascinating shoreline. From its dam, the lake extends south for about a mile, then forks into two branches. The southeast branch is wider and longer, but the southwest branch has more interesting coves.

The western shore is densely wooded, with numerous deep coves. Rolling hay fields border the east shore. We stayed until dusk and watched a glorious sunset cast its golden glow on this lovely pastoral setting. This lake is as pretty for its panoramic vistas as anything else.

Canada geese sometimes make pests of themselves by grazing lawns, parks, and golf courses.

Canada geese congregate in a large cove just west of the dam. This cove contains three small islands wooded with willow, sycamore, and spruce trees. A farm perches on the south shore of this cove, and several farm geese have apparently flocked together with the wild geese.

GETTING THERE: From Hanover, at the intersection of Route 94 and Route 116 (Broadway and Baltimore), drive south on Route 94 for 3.4 miles. Turn right (west) on Fairview Drive, go 1.6 miles, then turn left on Beck Mill Road. Drive 0.6 mile, turn left on Grand Valley Road, then make an immediate right into the access.

Pinchot Lake (Conewago Lake)

Size: 340 acres

RESTRICTIONS: nonpowered boats and electric motors only
MANAGING AGENCY: Gifford Pinchot State Park (2,338 acres)
LOCATION: between Maytown and Rossville, York County

This heavily developed lake between Harrisburg and York sees extensive use during the summer months. It's popular with the Baltimore-D.C. crowd. Long and narrow, Pinchot Lake stretches more than two miles south from its dam. Most suitable for wildlife watching is the extreme southern end of the lake, where it narrows, juts westward under Route 177, and opens into a wide, triangular-shaped lagoon. This area is worth the trip. We launched directly into this lagoon, at Launch Site No. 1.

Don't let the duckweed here scare you away from this biologically fascinating lagoon. Many people unknowingly call duckweed "pond scum." But duckweed isn't the least bit "scummy." Reassure yourself by scooping up a handful. Go ahead, it's really just millions of tiny, individual plants. Duckweed is among the tiniest flowering plants in the world. Notice the tiny, hairlike roots. These extract nutrients from the water. Duckweed is free-floating, which is why in areas with current it congregates in little nooks and crannies. The duckweed in this lagoon is so thick it gives the water a solid green appearance and actually creates drag as you paddle through it. Our canoe left no path as we moved northward; the tiny plants quickly closed up behind us. But we moved through it easily enough, enjoying the many wood ducks we encountered. We saw several family groups. Frogs jumped all around us, a green-backed heron crouched in the cattails, and everywhere we saw green, duckweed-covered turtles sunning on logs and rocks.

At the lagoon's north end, we slipped into Beaver Creek. We paddled upstream for about a half mile, surprised by how wide and accessible the creek was, and goaded on by the discoveries we made around every bend, such as the large muskrat we saw shortly after entering the creek. At first we hoped it was a beaver, since this was Beaver Creek, but we soon saw the long naked rattail moving side to side as the animal swam. And as large as it was, it was still only about one-quarter the size of a beaver. Eventually it disappeared below the water, between two large rocks along the shore. Farther on we saw two male wood ducks and another smaller muskrat. Deep woods surrounded us, and we heard scarlet tanagers and a wood thrush singing in the distance.

We paddled back to the launch, then headed east under the Route 177 bridge. From this skinny bottleneck, the lake widens rapidly. We headed for a marshy area at the lake's southern tip. Here we saw many families of wood ducks. There were woodies everywhere—sunning on the rocks, moving through the cattails, and swimming in the lake. Notable, we thought, was the absence of any nest boxes. Obviously they were nesting somewhere.

The state park offers two swimming beaches, canoe and rowboat rentals, 340 blacktopped campsites, ten rental cabins, and hiking trails. For more information, call the park office at 717-432-5011.

GETTING THERE: From I-83 north of York, take Exit 13 and head north on Route 382 for 3.9 miles to Route 177. Turn left (south) and go 3.9 miles to the park office. Continue south another 1.7 miles to Launch Site No. 1, on the right. *Or* from Harrisburg, take Exit 15 off of I-83 and head south on Route 177 for about 8 miles to the park.

Tuscarora Lake

Size: 96 acres

RESTRICTIONS: nonpowered boats and electric motors only
MANAGING AGENCY: Tuscarora State Park
LOCATION: near Barnesville, Schuylkill County

Tuscarora Lake lies in Locust Valley, at the southern end of the state's anthracite coal region. Unlike outlying areas, this valley was spared from coal mining and remains relatively pristine and unscarred.

The narrow lake stretches for about a mile from its east-end dam to its west-end headwaters, where it veers sharply south. There is a small swimming beach and picnic area on the north shore. Other than that, the lake is completely undeveloped. Locust Mountain rises from the south shore. Hemlocks, birch, and oaks meet the water's edge. Rhododendron thickets along the south shore are beautiful in early June bloom. In any season, the sweet, evergreen smell of hemlock permeates the air.

The narrow upper arm of Tuscarora Lake offers isolation, shade, and cool, crystal clear water.

We loved this lake and we promised ourselves to return for the fall colors. We found the crystal-clear water just great for fish watching, especially along the mouth of Locust Creek, at the lake's west end. Here we saw several large catfish and some largemouth bass. It's possible to paddle several hundred yards up into the narrow arm at the lake's headwaters. And the trip is well worth the effort. Here, well away from swimmers and fishermen, wedged between the mountains, it's possible to feel isolated and alone. We ate lunch on a large boulder overhanging the water and waded in the creek, reveling in the solitude.

Paddling back to the launch, we witnessed a curious incident. A wild turkey stepped from the shadows of the hemlocks on the south shore and began drinking from the lake. We've seen lots of wild turkeys, but never from a canoe. It just struck us as a bit peculiar. But actually, turkeys need a steady supply of fresh drinking water. Water is one of the key requirements of quality turkey habitat.

The single launch on this lake is tucked into a cove on the northeast end, near the dam. It's accessible twenty-four hours per day. Canoes and other nonpowered boats can be rented at a concession on the north shore, near the swimming beach.

For more information, call the Tuscarora State Park office at 717-467-2404.

NEARBY: The fifty-two-acre Locust Lake, located in Locust Lake State Park, lies six miles west of Tuscarora Lake. This small, roundish lake has no coves or inlets to explore, but the shoreline is completely wooded, and mountains rise all around. Also, there are hiking trails and 282 wooded campsites, neither of which is available at Tuscarora. Canoe rentals are also available. Many area visitors use Locust Lake as a base camp and explore Tuscarora Lake and the surrounding environs from there. Additional hiking trails can be found in Weiser State Forest, which lies adjacent to Locust Lake State Park.

For more information about Locust Lake State Park, call the park office at 717-467-2404. The summer campground number is 717-467-2772.

GETTING THERE: From Tamaqua, take Route 309 North less than a mile from town, then bear left onto S.R. 1018 at the park sign. Drive 2.8 miles, then turn left at park entrance, then left again to launch.

From I-81, take the Mahanoy City/Hometown exit (37 East) and follow the signs to Tuscarora State Park. There are many turns, but the route is well marked.

Leaser Lake

Size: 117 acres

RESTRICTIONS: nonpowered boats and electric motors only
MANAGING AGENCY: Fish and Boat Commission
LOCATION: Jacksonville, Lehigh County
HOURS: 5:00 A.M.–10:00 P.M.

Leaser Lake lies nestled between Blue Mountain to its north and well-manicured farms and rolling fields to the south. The tiny, old village of Jacksonville is perched on the lake's east shore. The pastoral vistas from the canoe rival the scenery anywhere in the state.

The lake's best feature is its fascinating configuration. From its dam at the south end, the lake fans north in a series of large and small coves. A large, round island, along with the many coves, creates the impression of a seemingly endless series of channels and waterways. We had fun just exploring these "paths" and trying to figure out how they were all connected.

As a county park, Leaser Lake is more manicured and well maintained than most lakes. Much of the shoreline is open and mowed. A fairly large Canada goose population inhabits the area, and, apparently, the killdeer like the open shorelines, too.

When we canoed here in early summer of 1993, the lake was closed indefinitely to fishing, as it had recently been drained for dam repair, then refilled and stocked with fingerling fish. Canoeists and kayakers pretty much have this lake to themselves for the time being.

NEARBY: While in the area, be sure to visit the Hawk Mountain Sanctuary near Kempton, especially if you're there during the fall. You just might catch a wave of majestic hawks and eagles. The sanctuary also houses a first-rate nature center, art gallery, and gift shop.

GETTING THERE: From Route 309 between Allentown and Tamaquah, turn south on Route 143. Go 4.9 miles, turn right onto Ontelaunee Road (at sign for lake), and drive 0.9 mile. Turn left into parking lot and launch. Or continue another 0.3 mile on Route 143 and turn right onto Pleasure Court in the village of Jacksonville. This leads to a second launch on the lake's east side.

Canada Geese

The female Canada goose sat quietly incubating her clutch of five eggs. Her eyes followed the passersby who were too absorbed in thought or conversation to notice the nest even though it rested just a few feet off the busy park trail. I discovered the nest because I just happened to glance that way as the hen turned the eggs. Her movement caught my eye. I found a shady bench nearby and stopped to watch for awhile.

Finally a little boy strolled by. His eyes widened and a smile crossed his face. He saw the goose. He no doubt recognized the bird and thought it harmless. Even five-year-olds have seen pictures of Canada geese—large gray body, black neck and head, and a distinctive white chin strap that stretches from ear to ear. He approached the nest boldly, perhaps hoping to pet the big bird.

The goose, on the other hand, viewed the boy's approach as a threat. Though the goose had built its nest within the confines of a park, it was a wild bird. And the boy was an intruder. What followed happened so fast I didn't have time to warn the boy. A personal lesson would mean much more than a lecture from a stranger anyway. Just as the boy reached out to stroke the goose, it hissed and snapped its bill at his fingers. The boy turned and ran crying back to his parents, who were now just catching up to their curious and adventurous son. And none too soon. For right after the hen's attack, the male, who had been standing guard nearby, charged to the nest's defense, hissing and flailing its wings.

It was a classic case of geese defending their nest. Few animals protect their families more fiercely than Canada geese. No broken wing act for these birds. When they're threatened, they attack. Geese mate for life. They take their pair bond seriously and do whatever it takes to raise their brood. The hen incubates the eggs for about four weeks and defends the nest herself. The gander's job is to defend an area around the nest and drive off intruders before they get to the nest.

In Pennsylvania, that means running off raccoons, opossums, skunks, foxes, crows, and maybe an occasional bobcat or coyote. On the Arctic tundra, where most Canada geese nest, the task is more difficult. Discouraging a marauding raccoon is one thing, but fighting off a grizzly bear or a wolverine is quite another.

RJM

A protective papa goose, however, rarely retreats. He easily sends small predators on their way and readily attacks larger intruders. This is true of most geese, wild and domestic. One of my vivid childhood memories is being chased and flopped by the domestic geese every time I visited a relative's farm. This fierce protective behavior helps Canada geese establish strong family bonds. For unlike most birds, Canada geese stay together as family units for almost a full year.

As the days grow shorter in the fall, listen for the distinctive, "Honk, honk, honk" from a flock of geese passing southward overhead. Gaze skyward and look for the familiar **V**. These flocks aren't just random assemblies of birds. Most consist of family groups— sets of parents and their young of the year that survived to flight stage. And sometimes older, nonbreeding young rejoin their parents for the return flight to the winter area. They fly to the parents' traditional winter range, perhaps Virginia or the Carolinas. Come spring, they'll return again as a family. En route the young learn the way by some combination of visual, celestial, or perhaps even geomagnetic cues.

Only after returning to the breeding grounds does the extended family group break up. Nonbreeding one- and two-year-olds stay together and search for a hospitable summer home where they can avoid territorial nesting adults. Their journey may take them hundreds of miles from their birthplace. This is how young geese disperse and eventually meet unrelated potential mates. In the company of all those new faces, the search for a life mate begins.

Though most Canada geese nest in the Arctic, not all nest so far north. Many have adapted well to human disturbance and nest throughout the continent on wildlife areas, parks, farms, cemeteries, and golf courses. Most states now have local breeding populations of Canada geese, and Pennsylvania is no exception. In fact, as you paddle the state's quiet waters, you will probably find Canada geese at every lake. In some areas they graze on mowed areas like domestic fowl. Elsewhere you'll spot them in the remotest corner of a marsh.

Like any wild creature that lives in close association with humans, Canada geese can be annoying, even a nuisance. They graze well-manicured parks, yards, golf courses, and newly sprouted farm fields, leaving behind their malodorous and messy calling cards. Just the presence of large numbers of geese can turn beautiful landscapes into mud holes. Sometimes they even chase and attack children.

Times and circumstances have twisted the image of Canada geese in some quarters from a magnificent bird into an undesirable pest. But whose fault is that? Nesting platforms encourage breeding all across the state. You'll see them at many of the lakes we recommend in this book. On one hand, we welcome them and manage the popluation to increase its size; on the other, we complain when management succeeds. Perhaps goose management decisions should be based on what's best for geese and the general public rather than what's best for goose hunters.

To those who understand their natural history, Canada geese remain a symbol of all that is wild and free. Each spring and fall their trademark V formations and unrestrained honking stir the spirit and soothe the soul. May their call of the wild echo across the land forever.

South-Central Region

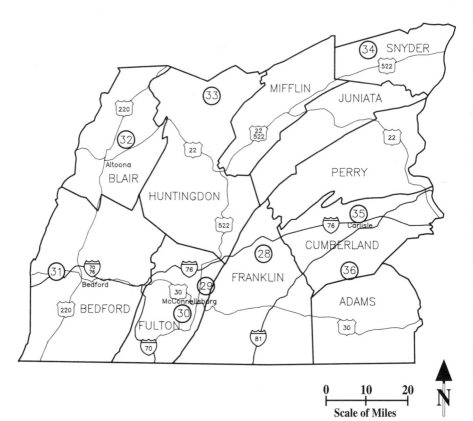

28. *Letterkenny Reservoir*

29. *Cowans Gap Lake*

30. *Meadow Grounds Lake*

31. *Shawnee Lake*

32. *Canoe Lake*

33. *Stone Valley Lake*

34. *Walker Lake*

35. *Opossum Lake*

36. *Laurel Lake*

Appalachian mountain ridges and valleys characterize Pennsylvania's south-central region. From Blue Mountain north of Carlisle, this region dips and swells its way south to the Maryland border. Mountainous Michaux State Forest covers much of the area. And farms dot the region, many of them owned by the Amish, who are expanding westward into the area's tillable mountain valleys.

Two major highways, U.S. Route 30 and the Pennsylvania Turnpike (I-76) cross the rural, often rugged region. Both are scenic highways. The turnpike tunnels under four mountains here. Route 30 passes by many historical sites, including Gettysburg National Military Park and Old Bedford Village, a reconstructed pioneer village.

The gentle Juniata River passes through the northern part of this region. Canoeists can enjoy a 30-mile "quiet" paddle from Route 103 bridge in Lewistown to the Route 17 bridge in Millerstown. The river along here passes through high ridges.

Farther south the Juniata River is dammed to form the 8,300-acre Raystown Lake. Motorboating is unrestricted on this 30-mile long lake, but canoeists may wish to explore the extensive fingers and coves of the northwest shoreline.

Letterkenny Reservoir

Size: 54 acres

RESTRICTIONS: nonpowered boats and electric motors only
MANAGING AGENCY: Fish and Boat Commission
LOCATION: near Roxbury, Franklin County

Just to get to this mountain lake requires a drive through mountain valleys and past Amish farms and rolling fields. Then there is the climb up
steep, winding roads. By the time we got there, we were expecting
great things. And we weren't disappointed. Nestled between Kittatinny
and Blue mountains, surrounded by extensive state game lands, Letterkenny Reservoir lies in a steep, wooded mountain valley. From its
dam, the lake runs southwest for about three-quarters of a mile. The
dam abuts a dramatic rocky outcrop. Letterkenny Reservoir serves as
the water source for Letterkenny Army Depot near Roxbury, to the
south.

Unless you visit here on the opening day of trout season, chances
are you'll have this lake to yourself. We did. We launched from the
west shore and headed south. The water is clear and very deep in the
center of the lake. Inlets through the sedges and alder thickets characterize the south end, and we paddled toward the largest inlet in the
extreme southwest corner. The water here becomes shallow, with many
submerged tree stumps. We found large gelatinous colonies of *Pectinella magnifica,* a common freshwater bryozoan, attached to many of
these stumps. We also found an uprooted maple tree that had fallen into
the water. We could see how porcupines had eaten away the bark from
the higher limbs. Porcupines' bark-eating habit often damages or
destroys trees. Typically, they sit high in a tree close to the trunk, eating
bark, twigs, and leaves. When a tree trunk is completely girdled, the
tree dies.

At the reservoir's southeast corner, we paddled into Conodoquinet
Creek. For several hundred yards the creek runs wide and deep. We
saw several large bass. But then the water became too shallow, and we
turned back into the lake.

Beavers maintain an active colony on the lake. Paddling north now
and hugging the east shore, we found the largest beaver lodge we ever
saw in Pennsylvania. It was much larger in diameter than our seventeen-foot canoe, and we estimated that it stood at least six feet high.

Letterkenny Reservoir nestles in a steeply wooded mountain valley between Kittatinny and Blue mountain.

When we approached for a closer look, we discovered as much wood under the water as above it. The lodge extended well out into the deep water surrounding the above-water portion, which was anchored to the shore. Felled trees and pointed stumps blanketed the shoreline. A classic scene!

According to a local fisherman we met later, the reservoir supports a healthy population of trout and big bass. But he warned us about the heavy evening fog that can settle over this mountaintop lake in minutes, trapping boaters and anglers who aren't paying attention.

GETTING THERE: From the Pennsylvania Turnpike take Exit 14 (Willow Hill) and head north on Route 75 for 4.5 miles. Turn right on Route 641 East, go 6.5 miles, then make a hard right turn at sign for lake. Drive 0.4 mile to reservoir access road and another 0.4 mile to launch. *Or* from Pennsylvania Turnpike take Exit 15 (Blue Mountain) and drive south on Route 997 for 4 miles. Turn west on S.R. 641. Drive 2.5 miles, bear left at reservoir sign, drive 0.4 mile to reservoir access road, and another 0.4 mile to launch.

Cowans Gap Lake

Size: 42 acres

RESTRICTIONS: nonpowered boats and electric motors only
MANAGING AGENCY: Cowans Gap State Park (1,085 acres)
LOCATION: near McConnellsburg, Fulton County

This small, developed mountain lake makes an ideal location for beginners and families whose young children want to paddle. On this small lake, which lacks any coves or inlets, the kids will be in sight the whole time they are canoeing. Yet forty-two acres gives them room to maneuver. And the rest of the family can swim or lounge at lakeside picnic tables, enjoying the wooded setting.

Located in the foothills of the Tuscarora Mountains, the park area has an interesting history. It is named for Major Samuel Cowan, a British officer during the revolutionary war who eloped with the daughter of a Boston merchant. On their way from Chambersburg to Kentucky, the couple's wagon broke down and they traded it to Indians for the land now called Cowans Gap.

Rowboats and paddleboats can be rented on the lake. And there are many miles of trails in both the state park and adjacent 70,242-acre Buchanan State Forest. Some trails are steep and rocky, requiring good physical conditioning. Before hiking, be sure to find out about trail conditions from the park office. The park offers 258 campsites and ten family cabins, available spring, summer, and fall. The Civilian Conservation Corps constructed these cabins in 1937, as well as the lake itself, the park roads, and the picnic shelters. The cabins are listed on the National Register of Historic Places.

Cowans Gap is a great place to pitch a tent for a week or so, let the family gain experience maneuvering a canoe, and thoroughly hike the extensive network of trails through a wild and wooded mountainous region. The park gets heavy summertime use, so avoid peak season.

For more information, call the park office at 717-485-3948.

GETTING THERE: From U.S. 30 east of McConnellsburg, turn left (north) onto Aughwick Road at Tuscarora Summit and sign for state park. Go 6.4 miles to park office and visitor center. Turn left at park office to boat launch. *Or* from U.S. 30 west of Chambersburg, take

Route 75 north for about 4.5 miles, then turn left (west) onto Richmond Road at park sign. Drive 3.2 miles to the park. *Or* from the Pennsylvania Turnpike, take Exit 14 (Willow Hill) and drive south on Route 75 for 14.2 miles, then turn right (west) onto Richmond Road at park sign and proceed 3.2 miles to the park.

Meadow Grounds Lake

Size: 204 acres

RESTRICTIONS: nonpowered boats and electric motors only
MANAGING AGENCY: Fish and Boat Commission
LOCATION: near McConnellsburg, Fulton County

Meadow Grounds Lake, long, narrow, and beautiful, is tucked in the middle of state game lands high on Meadow Grounds Mountain. From the south-end dam, the lake stretches due north. An otherwise lovely view of the conifer/deciduous forest surrounding the lake is marred by a distinct band of dead trees all along the west shoreline, about 100 yards back from the water. These trees obviously are the victims of insect damage, probably exotic gypsy moths.

Cattails, jewelweed, sedges, buttonbush, and other marshy vegetation rings the shoreline. The lake's north end narrows into tiny, marshy coves sheltering wood duck boxes and geese nesting platforms. We also passed an open field along the middle of the west shore. This, we suspect, is a habitat management area. On an evening jaunt you could expect to see deer or even a bear in this field.

An eerie band of skeletal trees lines the shore of Meadow Grounds Lake, grim evidence of recent gypsy moth damage.

A pair of Tiger Swallowtails "puddles" along the shore of Meadow Grounds Lake, sipping essential minerals dissolved in the mud.

As we were launching from the east shore on an early summer afternoon, we noticed a congregation of tiger swallowtails clustered on the muddy launch ramp. We've seen this phenomenon several times before along a small stream near our home. The butterflies apparently extract mineral salts from the soil.

As we canoed, the peaceful silence of the lake was broken only by birds singing from shoreline trees and great blue herons squawking overhead (we flushed several). High on a mountain like this, a breeze blows almost constantly. This can produce a current and choppy waters that can give canoeists a good workout. We were tired after our exploration of the 1.5 mile-long lake.

GETTING THERE: From Pennsylvania Turnpike Exit 12 (Breezewood), take Route 30 east for 15.7 miles (2 miles west of McConnellsburg). Just as Route 30 becomes a divided highway, turn left at a large lake sign. Go 1 mile, then turn right onto S.R. 1003 at sign for state game lands. Drive 1 mile, turn right onto Meadow Grounds Road (at lake sign). Proceed 1.8 miles on mostly rough dirt road to the launch. A second launch is located 0.5 mile farther.

Shawnee Lake

Size: 451 acres

RESTRICTIONS: nonpowered boats and electric motors only
MANAGING AGENCY: Shawnee State Park (3,983 acres)
LOCATION: near Schellsburg, Bedford County

Shawnee Lake ranks among our top ten Pennsylvania lakes. Named for the Shawnee Indians who lived briefly in this area in the early 1700s, during their westward emigration, the lake offers a fascinating configuration and countless canoeing adventures. From the east-end dam, the lake extends west about 1.5 miles, then branches northeast and southwest another half mile each way. A large cove near the dam reaches northward. A large island in the middle divides the lake into three major sections, all connected by narrow channels. Lake development—a swimming beach, boat rental, and picnic areas—is confined to the north shore of the east section. Woodlots interspersed with marsh characterize the remaining shorelines.

We launched from the west end, just off Route 96, and headed due west and immediately under the Route 96 bridge. This structure hosts a large colony of barn and cliff swallows. We got a good, close look at the nests, nestlings, and adult birds. Past the bridge we proceeded west into a small, marshy lagoon at the headwaters of Shawnee Branch. Wood ducks were everywhere. And we had our best look ever at a green-backed heron when one perched in a willow tree as we passed directly underneath. The bird never moved. Rusty neck, bright yellow legs, dark green back—we could see it all, even its crest of feathers not usually visible from a distance.

We continued west into Shawnee Branch for several hundred yards. The water here is clear and cold, and we saw a brook trout resting in the shade of an overhanging bush. We turned around when we came to some impassable riffles, but you could easily portage past them. In fact, it would be fun to paddle or even wade (depending on water levels) another 200 or 300 yards to a covered bridge over the creek.

But we had an entire lake to explore. Out under the Route 96 bridge again, we headed south through a small, dredged channel and entered the lake's southwest section. This section extends west under another Route 96 bridge (more swallows) and narrows into a beautiful,

A white-tailed deer on the far edge of the cattails at Shawnee Lake is visible only to quiet water paddlers.

marshy area of cattails, sedges, and water lilies. As we entered the area, we startled a buck in velvet standing far out among the water lilies. He watched us briefly, then slowly waded back through the cattails and into the surrounding woods. White-tailed deer apparently like marshy areas. We see many as we canoe Pennsylvania's lakes.

We flushed a large flock of wood ducks at the inlet of Kegg Run. The inlet was clogged with water lilies when we visited, but depending on water level and time of year, it may be possible to paddle into the run a short way.

We headed east, back under the Route 96 bridge, and paddled close to a mile to the lake's large eastern section. A bridge from the south shore to the island separates the southwestern and eastern sections. As we passed under the bridge we saw the regional park office housed on the island. The white barn, outbuildings, and houses are all that's left of a dairy farm that once operated where the lake now lies.

We explored the lake's south shore, near the dam, then turned back west again to paddle under another bridge connecting the island with the lake's northwest section, thus completing our circle of the island and the lake. Along the island's north shore, look for kingfishers nesting in the holes they excavate on the high dirt banks. We passed two smaller, wooded islands just before we reached the west-end launch.

It was a long but wonderful trip. The wildlife and scenic vistas as we explored the inlets and circled the large island made the hours of paddling worthwhile.

The park features twelve miles of hiking trails, a swimming beach, boat rentals, 265 camping sites, and picnic areas.

For more information, call the park office at 814-733-4218.

NEARBY: Just east of the park is Old Bedford Village, a reconstructed colonial village featuring real buildings collected from around the county. The city of Bedford Historic District offers a walking tour of fifty-one historical buildings. Scenic Route 30, which roughly parallels Forbes Trail, skirts the park's north edge. This trail linked Fort Bedford and Fort Ligonier and passes many old buildings and inns as it winds through the countryside. One inn we visited was the Jean Bonnet Tavern, built about 1760 and listed on the National Register of Historic Places. This tavern now functions as a bed-and-breakfast inn and a fine dining establishment. For information, call innkeeper Lynn Baer at 814-623-2250.

GETTING THERE: From U.S. 30 in Schellsburg, west of Bedford, take Route 96 south for 0.7 mile to the west-end launch. The park office is another 1.2 miles south on Route 96. There's another launch on the north shore, near the swimming beach and day-use area.

Canoe Lake

Size: 155 acres

RESTRICTIONS: nonpowered boats and electric motors only
MANAGING AGENCY: Canoe Creek State Park (958 acres)
LOCATION: near Canoe Creek, Blair County

Canoe Lake may look a little dull at first—a big, open, circular lake. But there's more here than meets the eye. Located near a historic limestone kiln due east of Altoona, Canoe Lake lies in an area of rich limestone deposits. From its dam, the lake extends northeastward, gradually tapering into the marshy inlet of Canoe Creek.

We launched and headed north, away from the lake's developed south end. Numerous submerged logs and tree stumps make paddling a bit tricky at the northeast end, but we wanted to proceed gently anyway. We wanted to watch the feeding herons and sneak up on the countless painted turtles resting on logs.

On a tiny mudflat we noticed what looked like two little black-and-white chicks bobbing around on the mud. We floated closer and were startled by a loud squawk as a large bird appeared and flopped on the mud. Instantly we understood. The chicks were killdeer fledglings, and a parent was pulling the old broken wing routine to draw us away. What an act!

Nearby a small flock of cedar waxwings perched on emergent tree stumps. Several of the birds held something white in their beaks. Through our binoculars we could see they were eating white moths. We decided they must be eating the adult moth form of the elm spanworm. Like gypsy moths, spanworms periodically infest Pennsylvania forests. In 1993 infestation was particularly heavy in the northwestern quadrant of the state. Defoliated trees and white moths littering the forest floor were common sights.

The lake becomes quite shallow here, but it's usually possible to reach Canoe Creek. We explored well upstream, amazed by the beaver evidence all around us—felled trees, burrows riddling the banks, and a large lodge. Finally, we were forced to stop at a large beaver dam. Judging by the fresh-cut branches on the top, the beavers had worked on the dam that morning! We beached the canoe and waded in the clear, cold water, cameras in tow. Suddenly, *slap!* A beaver startled us with a warning tail slap, and we almost lost our footing. It disappeared behind the dam just as quickly as it had appeared.

Later, we saw more beaver evidence in the lake's northwest corner, near the boat rental concession at the inlet of Mary Ann's Creek. Here again the shallow water almost stymied us. But we found a channel and got through to the creek. Along the creek banks we saw several large holes that could easily have been beaver dens. In some areas, beavers forgo lodges for burrows in the banks of creeks or streams.

As you canoe this lake, don't forget to enjoy the vistas. The largely open shoreline affords a wonderful view of the hills and farm fields nestling the lake.

Canoes, rowboats, and paddleboats can be rented at a concession on the west shore. There's also a swimming beach, a food concession, picnic areas, and hiking trails. No campsites are available, but there are eight modern rental cabins.

For more information, call the park office at 814-695-6807.

GETTING THERE: From Altoona, go east on Route 22 for 11.3 miles, turn left (north) at park sign onto Turkey Valley Road, then drive 0.6 mile and turn right to park office. To get to the launch, along the east shore, go back out to the park entrance and turn left, continuing east, on Route 22. Drive 0.3 mile, bear left onto Beaver Dam Road, and go 0.4 mile to access on the left.

Killdeer

It's always risky to guarantee that someone will see a particular animal if they go to a particular place at a particular time. I'd probably predict great blue herons and Canada geese at just about any Pennsylvania lake between May and September. But if I wanted to be absolutely certain not to disappoint an enthusiastic beginner, I'd promise them a killdeer. From March through October, killdeer can be found along the shores of just about every lake in the state.

Fortunately, killdeer are easy to identify, even for beginners. A member of the plover family, this common shorebird is ten to eleven inches long. Two black horizontal bands cross a white chest, and up close the adult's bright red eye is apparent. Many people already know the killdeer because of its peculiar habit of nesting right out in the open. Often it makes a scrape in a gravel driveway, parking lot, or even a neatly mown backyard. Its eggs look like large, mottled pebbles and are surprisingly difficult to find. This I know from experience.

A few years ago, while I was teaching a class in field ecology, a group of students marched into my office and threw down a challenge. They said they had something to show me at a nearby cemetery. So off we went. After a short walk, one of the students announced that I was now within sight of a killdeer nest. "This is our test for you. You have five minutes to find the nest."

I had found several killdeer nests in the past, but none had been easy. Even though killdeer nest in open areas—lakeshores, cultivated fields, airports, yards, driveways, parking lots and even flat, gravel rooftops—I knew I had my work cut out for me. The incubating parent sits low and tight and is difficult to see even on a freshly mown lawn. The biggest clue in finding the nest, I knew, would be the bird's behavior. So, hoping to get the bird's attention, I began walking back and forth across the area the students had pointed out.

After about two minutes, an alarm sounded. I turned around to see a killdeer flopping around on the ground not twenty feet away, acting as if its wing was broken. Its two alarm calls— "dee, dee" and "kill-dee"—were loud and piercing. Clearly the bird was calling attention to itself. The "broken wing act" draws the attention of predators away from the nest and to the "injured" adult.

I knew that an adult would not begin its act right at the nest. When alarmed, a killdeer slips off the nest and begins performing only when it judges itself to be a safe distance from the nest. I slowly approached the bird and noted the spot where I first saw it. As I got closer, the killdeer moved farther away, still dragging its wing. With each step, the bird lured me farther away from the original spot. After it had moved about fifty feet, it flew off and circled overheard. Its "kill-dee" calls (hence the bird's name) almost sounded like laughter, as if the bird was mocking me for being fooled.

But, being no ordinary predator, I returned to the spot I had first seen the bird and slowly began searching. I walked carefully because I knew the scrape of a nest and its mottled eggs are nearly impossible to see until you know where they are. And nothing would have been more embarrassing or reckless than to step on the nest in front of my students. Finally, with about twenty seconds to spare, I found the nest. The four large eggs, pointed end facing to the middle of the nest, resembled four equal-sized pieces of pie. The students seemed as pleased as I was.

Over the next few weeks we visited the nest every few days. But we used binoculars to observe from a distance so we wouldn't needlessly disturb the nest. The parents took turns incubating the eggs for twenty-six days. Within an hour after hatching, four alert, downy chicks scampered off with mom and dad. The family stayed together for about five weeks until the young could fly. Then they joined a flock of other killdeer at the edge of a nearby lake.

Killdeer usually return from their winter grounds in early March. In 1993 I saw my first killdeer of the year the day before the big March blizzard struck. How they survived two feet of snow, single-digit temperatures, and relentless winds is one of those natural wonders that never ceases to amaze me. It's almost as bewildering as how they can raise their broods in such open, unprotected habitat.

Stone Valley Lake

Size: 72 acres

RESTRICTIONS: nonpowered boats and electric motors only
MANAGING AGENCY: Pennsylvania State University's Stone
  Valley Recreation Area (700 acres)
LOCATION: near Petersburg, Huntingdon County
FEE: $16.35 seasonal-use permit

Pennsylvania State University owns and operates this beautiful little lake and recreation area in the Rothrock State Forest. Stone Valley Lake exists to promote wildlife conservation and appreciation for natural areas. Canoeists are encouraged to explore the lake's marshy coves and inlets, and interpretive programs are regularly offered, including a new Moonlight Canoe Program, where participants paddle at night to observe beavers and other nocturnal animals.

From its dam, the lake extends northeast, forking at the far end. Two coves along the west shore attract waterfowl and wildlife watchers alike. The main boat launch is located on the east shore at the Mineral Industries Day-Use Area. Canoes, rowboats, and sailboats can be rented here as well. A second launch, suitable only for boats not on a trailer, is located on the west shore. The lake is open for boating from April through October. Eleven year-round rental cabins are located just east of the lake.

For more information, call the main office, located on the Penn State campus, at 814-863-0762.

NEARBY: North of the lake lies Shaver's Creek Environmental Center, an integral feature of the Stone Valley Recreation Area. This superb facility exists "to provide exemplary environmental experiences that develop and nurture a respect and reverence for our Earth," according to the center's brochure. Interpretive and hands-on natural and cultural history exhibits can be found inside the center, while outside are the wildflower gardens and the Raptor Center. We were most impressed by the collection of live hawks, owls, and eagles—all injured birds that had been rehabilitated but could not be released into the wild. The Raptor Center conducts educational programs with these birds, and we attended one on the golden eagle, complete with the center's director handling the bird for us to see. A hiking trail links the Environmental

Center with the lake. Or you can drive there. For more information, call the Environmental Center, Penn State Campus, at 814-863-2000.

Another site to visit while you're in the area is Whipple Lake. This twenty-two-acre lake in Whipple Dam State Park is just about three miles east of Stone Valley, off Route 26. It affords an easy hour or two of canoeing and rounds out a visit to Stone Valley Lake.

From the west shore launch, we headed north into a shallow, marshy area filled with sedges, grasses, and cattails. We saw spotted sandpipers on some exposed mudflats and almost got stuck in the mud. This north end is pretty badly silted in, but we worked our way to the east shore, past the swimming beach, and found a deep channel leading to Laurel Run. We headed upstream for some distance, noting the beaver-notched trees and fallen logs, until we were stopped by a huge beaver dam. We beached the canoe and waded around the dam, marveling at the fluorescent green damselflies lighting all over the dam. There were dozens of them! Laurel Run meanders through deep woods and is a beautiful place to hike or explore. And there are countless

Linda takes notes after an early morning paddle.

opportunities for hiking and scenic drives through the adjacent Rothrock State Forest.

Also nearby: Historic Boalsburg, just east of State College, site of the Boal Mansion and Museum, the Columbus Chapel, and a restored village of nineteenth-century Victorian homes and businesses. Several of the homes are now wonderful bed-and-breakfast establishments. One we recommend from personal experience is the Summer House. For information, call Summer House at 814-466-3304.

GETTING THERE: From State College, take Route 26 south to intersection with Route 45. Continue south on Route 26 for 5.7 miles. Turn right onto S.R. 1029, drive 1.8 miles, then turn left at sign onto access road and left again at the next fork (following signs) and go 1.6 miles to launch. Turning right at the fork will take you to Shaver's Creek Environmental Center.

Walker Lake

Size: 239 acres

RESTRICTIONS: nonpowered boats and electric motors only
MANAGING AGENCY: Fish and Boat Commission
LOCATION: near Troxelville, Snyder County

Canoeing Walker Lake requires a special effort. It's not on the way to anywhere. Of course, its isolation is one of this lake's nicest features. Nestled between Jack's and Penn's Creek mountains to the north and Shade Mountain to the south, Walker Lake lies long and narrow on the valley floor. Paddle its two-mile length a few times for a good aerobic workout. On the day we visited, a strong south wind blew hard and we worked up a good sweat.

A narrow band of cattails and small trees rims the north shore and gives that side of the lake a marshy look. The mountains looming in the background to the north add an air of wilderness to the experience. Mallards, three great blue herons, a great egret, and a green-backed heron foraged along the shallow shoreline as we paddled past. The great blues seemed almost playful. They stayed about fifty yards in front of us as we worked our way from southwest to northeast.

The south shore, on the other hand, is densely wooded with oaks, hemlocks, maples, hickories, and dogwood. We saw no waterbirds on this side of the lake, probably because the shoreline drops off quickly so there are no shallow spots to wade and feed. But we spent a few minutes "pishing and squeaking" on this side of the lake and roused five species. Several black-capped chickadees, two red-eyed vireos, a scarlet tanager, an eastern phoebe, and a downy woodpecker responded to the sound of a potential territorial intruder.

Our birding experience at Walker Lake suggests that it might be a real hot spot in late April and early May. A good strategy would be to scan the marshy north shore for waterfowl and waders and bird the more wooded south shoreline for songbirds. And don't be surprised to find a loon and/or a few grebes here during spring and fall migration.

NEARBY: While you're in the neighborhood, check out Faylor Lake just north of Beaver Springs. At least nine small islands dot this picturesque little lake, which sits among a mosaic of cultivated fields, wooded hillsides, and distant mountains.

GETTING THERE: Take Route 235 north from Beaver Springs to Troxelville. When Route 235 turns hard to the north to leave Troxelville, continue straight for 1 mile. Then turn right at the Fish Commission sign for Walker Lake. Continue 1 more mile to the parking lot and boat launch.

Opossum Lake

Size: 59 acres

RESTRICTIONS: nonpowered boats and electric motors only
MANAGING AGENCY: Fish and Boat Commission
LOCATION: near Carlisle, Cumberland County

This little gem north of Carlisle sits against a backdrop of majestic Blue Mountain to the north. The lake stretches long and narrow from its dam at the south end to the marshy northern reaches. The west shoreline is entirely wooded and very irregular, with several large coves near the north end. Herons tend to frequent these coves. Another long, narrow cove at the south end juts eastward. On the east, the shoreline is wooded along the northern half and open along the southern half, except for a large pine grove near the dam. Bird boxes stand all along the west shore, presumably for tree swallows or prothonotary warblers. We didn't see any.

Rural residences and cultivated fields dot the countryside surrounding the lake. But on the lake itself, it's easy to feel alone and isolated. We had the waters to ourselves, except for a few Canada geese and mallards.

Opossum Lake is one of the better examples of a Fish Commission lake. Here, as at some other "shining stars" such as Long Arm Dam, we found no litter and clean, unspoiled water. Unfortunately, our experience would indicate that this is the exception rather than the rule. Most Fish Commission lakes are littered with Styrofoam bait cups, tangles of monofilament line, and beer and soda cans. Some people might be tempted to form stereotypes about the typical American fisherman. A State Game Commission employee told us about the miles and miles of trout streams no longer accessible to the public because landowners simply could no longer tolerate the littering and disregard for personal property. Backpackers and primitive campers have always packed out their trash. Why can't fishermen? Perhaps the littering problem could be curbed if the Fish Commission at least provided trash cans at each lake. We saw only one lake with a trash can, and that was in the pit toilet stall. This, of course, would require the commission to pay employees to empty and monitor those cans, and it would assume that at least some fishermen would make the effort to use the cans. Perhaps some of the extensive sums used to purchase new lakes could be channeled into maintaining the ones already owned.

GETTING THERE: From Carlisle, drive north on Route 74 (Waggoner's Gap Road) for 2 miles past the Pennsylvania Turnpike, then turn left (west) onto Easy Road. Drive 3.3 miles to Opossum Lake Road. Turn right, then make a quick left onto access road. This is the most direct route. Ignore the lake signs in downtown Carlisle. They are misleading and incomplete and will get you dreadfully lost. We know.

Belted Kingfishers

We had barely launched the canoe when a machine-gun-like rattle echoed along the lakeshore. A kingfisher soared by, rattling as it flew. It lit on a bare branch about a hundred yards ahead of us.

A few minutes later the kingfisher demonstrated why it is aptly named. It took off and flew our way. Before reaching us, it pulled up and hovered about twenty feet above the water. For several seconds the bird beat its wings furiously and held its posi-

tion in the air. All the while it eyed the water intently. Suddenly it folded its wings, plunged into the water, and disappeared completely beneath the surface. Moments later it emerged from the stream, minnow in bill, and returned to its perch. The kingfisher whacked the small fish senseless on the branch. Then it flipped its dinner into the air and swallowed it headfirst. Small fish less than four inches long make up more than half of the kingfisher's diet. Other prey include tadpoles, crayfish, insects, frogs, and small snakes and small turtles.

Found near lakes, streams, and rivers, belted kingfishers are common all across the state. And they are easy to identify, so you need not be a bird-watcher to recognize them. Their large (nine to twelve inches) blue-gray bodies contrast with white throats and bellies. A wide blue-gray "belt" crosses the chest. Females also wear a chestnut-colored band across the middle of their bellies. A long, pointed bill and prominent crest give kingfishers a distinctive bigheaded silhouette.

The nesting biology of kingfishers is as interesting as their feeding habits. Like woodpeckers, kingfishers nest in holes. But instead of chiseling holes in wood, kingfishers dig their cavities in exposed banks of streams, lakes, gravel pits, and road cuts. Nests may be several miles from water if feeding grounds lack suitable embankments. Both sexes take turns digging the nest hole. They dig with their bills and kick the dirt out with their feet. The tunnel to the nest chamber is about four inches in diameter and usually three to six feet long. It ends in a large circular nesting chamber the size and shape of a flattened, half-inflated basketball. The entire excavation takes about two or three weeks.

If the burrow has been used in years past, the floor may be littered with fish scales and bones. Kingfishers, like owls, regurgitate pellets of indigestible body parts after dining.

The female lays five to eight white eggs on the unlined floor of the nest chamber. Both parents share incubation duties. The eggs hatch about twenty-four days after the last one was laid. Kingfishers raise only one brood per year, but they renest repeatedly if early nests are destroyed by predators or rising water.

Young kingfishers remain in the nest until they are about a month old and able to fly. They stay near the nest burrow the first few days after fledging and watch their parents fish. Parent kingfishers use an interesting technique to teach their offspring how to fish. Often adults catch a fish, beat the life out of it on a perch, then drop it back into the water. This enables young kingfishers to practice fishing for prey that cannot swim away. Even this, however, can be a challenge the first time out. But young, hungry kingfishers learn quickly. In just a few days juveniles begin fishing for live prey on their own. Within two weeks of fledging, young kingfishers are fairly independent. They remain that way for most of their lives—belted kingfishers are loners except during the breeding season.

Next time you're out paddling and take your rod and reel along, listen for a peculiar rattling sound. When you hear it, you'll know a kingfisher's on patrol and the fishing's probably good. After all, where there are little fish, there are usually big fish, too.

Laurel Lake

Size: 25 acres

RESTRICTIONS: nonpowered boats and electric motors only
MANAGING AGENCY: Pine Grove Furnace State Park (696 acres)
LOCATION: near Mt. Holly Springs, Cumberland County

Located deep in the mountains of Michaux State Forest, little Laurel Lake scored big with us. This small lake provides a wonderful family canoeing experience and is just plain fun. Of course, the incredibly beautiful and isolated mountain setting only enhances the lake's appeal. Route 233 climbs a steep mountain as it approaches the state park, so Laurel Lake is truly a mountain lake.

The lake is roughly triangular in shape, with the dam in the northeast corner, the boat launch in the northwest corner, and the lake narrowing to a point at the south end. A V-shaped island dominates the south end, creating two deep, narrow channels that run along the island's outer edges and meet at the base of the V, where Mountain Creek enters the lake.

We launched and headed south into the clear, cold waters of the western channel. A canopy of trees covers the channel, keeping it cool and dark. It felt like we were paddling through a tunnel. The water is fairly deep in some spots and is stained from the tannic acid of organic debris. The Fish Commission stocks Mountain Creek with trout, and we saw several large brookies. The clear water is certainly conducive to fish watching. It's also incredibly tempting on a hot day, and we passed two young men who apparently couldn't resist the urge to cool off in a deep swimming hole.

We reached Mountain Creek and headed upstream 300 or 400 yards before we reached an area off-limits to watercraft. (We never did find out why.) We turned around and took the east channel back into the main body of the lake, thus completing our circle around the island. The entire trip took less than an hour, but it was a lot of fun, and we can't wait to take the girls along next time.

Pine Grove Furnace State Park is one of several state parks developed around the site of an old iron furnace. The Pine Grove Furnace began operations in 1764 and today is registered as a National Historic Site. Laurel Lake supplied water to a nearby iron forge, and the 1.7-acre Fuller Lake, located west of Laurel Lake, was a former iron quarry

RJM

for the furnace. Swimming beaches are now located at both lakes, as are picnic areas. Canoes can be rented at Laurel Lake. There is also a bicycle rental, food concessions, and a park store. The park provides seventy-four year-round camping sites and several hiking trails, including a portion of the Appalachian Trail. The 84,912-acre Michaux State Forest, which surrounds the park, provides countless hiking and wildlife-watching opportunities.

For more information, call the park office at 717-486-7174.

GETTING THERE: From I-81 west of Harrisburg, take Exit 11 and head south on Route 233. Drive 8.3 miles to the park office. Turn left (east) onto Pine Grove Furnace/Hunters Run Road and drive another 1.8 miles to Laurel Lake. From points east (York, Gettysburg) take Route 30 west to Route 233 in Caledonia and drive north on Route 233 about 13 miles to the park office.

TIP: If you're approaching the park from Harrisburg and you have the time, take scenic Route 174, which eventually intersects with Route 233. This lovely drive through the countryside passes through Boiling Springs and roughly parallels the Yellow Breeches Creek, undoubtedly the finest trout fishing stream in Pennsylvania.

Southwest Region

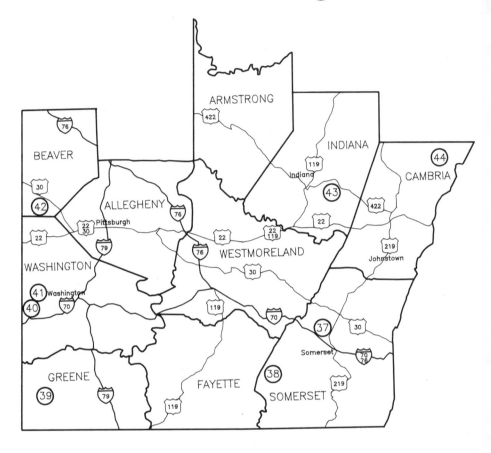

37. Lake Somerset
38. Cranberry Glade Lake
39. R.J. Duke Lake
40. Dutch Fork Lake
41. Cross Creek Lake
42. Racoon Lake
43. Yellow Creek Lake
44. Glendale Lake

The Laurel Highlands dominate Pennsylvania's southwest region. The Highlands cover more than 100 miles of Allegheny mountain and valley countryside and include the Laurel and Chestnut Ridges. Mountain laurel, the state flower, grows in abundance here. This "flower" is really an evergreen shrub, similar to rhododendron, that grows five to ten feet tall. Typically growing in dense stands, mountain laurel provides excellent cover for wildlife.

Three major rivers course through the southwest region: the Allegheny flows south, the Monongahela flows north, and they meet in Pittsburgh to form the mighty Ohio. The British established Fort Pitt at the junction of these rivers. During the French and Indian War, the French captured the fort and held it until it was recaptured by the British. Several battles were fought in the Laurel Highlands region, including those at Fort Necessity, Fort Ligonier, Bushy Run Battlefield, and Fort Pitt. George Washington saw his first military action in southwestern Pennsylvania at Fort Necessity.

A smaller river, the Youghiogheny (pronounced "Yock-i-gain-y"), flows north into the Monongahela. The Yough (pronounced "Yock") is a popular whitewater rafting and canoeing river, and recreational sites abound along its shores, including the large Ohiopyle State Park. George Washington tried to ship his men and their supplies along the Youghiogheny on his way to Fort Pitt but had to abandon his plans when he reached the famous waterfall now located within the state park.

Pittsburgh, of course, is the region's major urban center. We live only 75 miles from downtown Pittsburgh and visit her often. The most dramatic way to approach this beautiful city is on I-279 from the south, coming through the Fort Pitt Tunnel and entering the city at Point State Park. Hills and mountains cut off any view of the city until you emerge from the tunnel, then there it is, in all its rejuvenated glory: Three Rivers Stadium, the Carnegie Science Center, and Fort Pitt State Park on the left, Station Square on the right, and the city's skyscrapers straight ahead. Pittsburgh's "Golden Triangle" is one of urban America's grandest sights.

Lake Somerset

Size: 253 acres

RESTRICTIONS: nonpowered and electric motors only
MANAGING AGENCY: Fish and Boat Commission
LOCATION: Somerset, Somerset County

Lake Somerset, wedged between Routes 219 and 601 just northeast of Somerset, seems an unlikely spot for a significant wildlife event. Yet here in 1993, western Pennsylvania's second osprey nest since 1910 was discovered. We observed it on July 26. Another score for quiet water canoeing!

A shoreline mosaic of cattails, rolling fields, and woodlots hides the shopping centers and suburban sprawl surrounding this lake. And the distant hum of traffic reminds us of how close we are to the fast pace of daily life. It all faded into the background, though, when we paddled this beautiful lake and contemplated the magnificent raptors living and breeding here.

From its dam at the south end, the lake curves northward about 1.5 miles. A large cove juts eastward from the middle of the lake, and there, atop a tall pole platform, is where the ospreys constructed their large, bulky nest. We'd had a tip about the ospreys from a local man who reads Scott's syndicated nature column, and we were anxious to see them for ourselves.

We launched at the south-end access on the west shore. Heading east, we stopped just outside the cove, paddling only enough to keep from drifting. We could see one adult sitting upright on the nest and a smaller nestling beside it. Luck was with us that evening, and the adult suddenly left the nest, soaring over the lake and heading for the marshy north end dotted with tiny coves and numerous wood duck boxes. Even without binoculars we could see the identifying characteristics: a huge wingspan, with wings distinctly bent at the "elbows;" white face; white underside; and dark above. Suddenly, from about thirty feet above the water, the osprey pulled its wings back hard and dove. (This is called "stooping.") Its talons hit the water but came up empty. The bird began to soar again.

Ospreys eat fish exclusively. That's why they were so sensitive to DDT and the spraying of marshes and wetlands for mosquito control. Their comeback after the banning of DDT represents one of the greatest wildlife success stories.

Once again the osprey dived, and this time it came up with a small fish in its talons. Flying low over the lake, it headed for the nest and the waiting nestling. As we followed it with our binoculars, another adult osprey came into view. It was perched in a snag less than 100 yards north of the nest, just as plain as day. But we would never have noticed it if we hadn't been watching its mate fly right by it. The adult with the fish landed on the nest, and the ensuing flapping of wings and flurry of activity signaled feeding time, we presumed.

What a grand sight! In the hazy breeze of a humid summer evening, it was almost a religious experience. The steady hum of traffic on Route 219, not even one-quarter mile behind the nest, gave the experience an almost surreal quality.

Once again we were amazed at the incredible wildlife encounters possible in a canoe on lakes near major population centers.

GETTING THERE: From Exit 10 (Somerset) of the Pennsylvania Turnpike, follow signs to Route 281 North for 0.6 mile, turn left, and head north on Route 281 for 0.7 mile, then turn left at light and drive another 0.6 mile (you'll cross railroad tracks and pass the dam). Turn right at lake sign onto Fish Commission Road. Drive 0.5 mile to first launch. From here, there's a good view of the osprey nest across the lake. At the end of this road, turn right and drive 0.4 mile to second launch at south end of lake.

Cranberry Glade Lake

Size: 112 acres

RESTRICTIONS: nonpowered boats and electric motors only
MANAGING AGENCY: Fish and Boat Commission
LOCATION: near Scullton, Somerset County

One of the best features of Cranberry Glade Lake is getting there. Located in Somerset County's spectacularly scenic Laurel Highlands, the lake is accessible only by way of a "roller-coaster" ride on small country roads through rolling hills. From mid-May through the summer, look for bobolinks in the hay fields leading up to the lake.

According to the recently published *Atlas of Breeding Birds in Pennsylvania* (University of Pittsburgh Press, 1992), Somerset County is one of the state's hot spots for breeding bobolinks. This handsome member of the blackbird family nests in hay fields and meadows, but nesting is often thwarted when farmers cut the first hay crop. Males sport black bodies, a buffy nape, and large white shoulder and rump patches. They are most often seen perching on fences and flying across fields while singing their distinctively bubbly flight song.

The lake holds great promise, too. Largely surrounded by state game lands, Cranberry Glade Lake sits in a basin ringed by woods and rolling hay fields. The setting is simply lovely, and we found our eyes frequently drawn to the surrounding hills. There is no development aside from several small houses tucked back up on the access road that runs past the parking lot. From the dam at the south end, the lake extends northwest just over one-half mile. Unlike many Fish Commission lakes, this one was litter free. That may be because it is so isolated and receives few visitors.

Cranberry Glade Lake could be renamed "Water Lily Lake"; thick beds of yellow water lilies ring the shallow shoreline. Little Emma kept trying to pick the heavy, waxy yellow flowers as we moved through the beds. But the stems don't break easily. She almost tipped the canoe several times. We held one close so she could examine it. Coontail (an aquatic plant) flourishes here, too. In the water, individual plants stand erect and fluffy looking, like a raccoon's tail. But held in hand, the plant lies limp and scraggly.

A breeding area for ospreys and wood ducks occupies the lake's northwest corner and is off-limits to boats. All we saw there on a late afternoon in June, however, were tree swallows and starlings. Had we been there two years earlier we might have discovered western Pennsylvania's first osprey nest since 1910. In 1991 a pair of ospreys nested here. Two chicks were seen on June 15. Only one remained when Game Commission biologists returned on July 17 to band them.

Submerged stumps and fallen trees along the shore make this lake visually interesting and fun to explore. We moored beside one such fallen tree that our daughters begged to climb around on. While lounging "dockside" as the kids stretched their legs, we observed a beautiful little water snake. As we watched, the snake slithered from its sunning spot on a branch overhanging the water back into the base of the huge stump on shore.

Wherever you paddle in Pennsylvania's quiet waters you are likely to encounter water snakes. They eat small fish, frogs, and invertebrates and are an important cog in any wetland ecosystem. None is poisonous, so there's nothing to fear. But water snakes tend to be pugnacious and bite when provoked. So our advice is look but don't touch.

On the lake's tiny spillway, next to the parking area, water falls onto a stone walkway. We splashed in and walked through the shallow water to cool off on a hot day. You can also walk across the dam to wooded paths along the western shoreline.

Cranberry Glade Lake is one of our favorite spots and we recommend it highly.

GETTING THERE: From Confluence, take Route 281 North for 0.5 mile, turn left onto Groff Road, and proceed for 0.8 mile, then turn left onto Jersey Hollow Road (S.R. 3003), where there should be a sign for the lake. Proceed for 5.1 miles, then turn right onto Cranberry Road, at the lake sign. The lake is 2.3 miles from the turnoff. (The road turns to dirt halfway in.)

Wood Ducks

From late spring through mid-summer, wood ducks rank second only to Canada geese as Pennsylvania's most abundant waterfowl. We saw some, often many, at virtually every lake we visited. Today's abundance of wood ducks is the result of one of the biggest success stories in the history of wildlife management.

By the early 1900s woodies were rare, probably near extinction, over most of their range. Wood ducks nest in cavities found in large trees in swamps and along wooded rivers and streams. The destruction of mature bottomland forests, combined with market hunting for meat and feathers, nearly did them in. But thanks to the 1918 Migratory Bird Treaty Act between the U.S. and Canada and other forms of protection for the birds and their habitat, conservationists brought them back from the brink of oblivion. Today, they are common and widespread throughout the eastern United States.

A major reason wood ducks responded so well to conservation efforts is that, like bluebirds and wrens, wood ducks readily use man-made nest boxes. That's why you see dozens of large nest boxes on many of the state's public waterways. They may be rectangular wooden boxes or metal cylinders with cone-shaped roofs designed to deter hungry raccoons. Many people who have property on lakes or along streams and rivers build their own to help these spectacularly beautiful ducks. Building a wood duck box is fairly simple and requires only basic wood-working skills.

A wood duck box measures twelve by twelve inches square and about twenty-four inches high. It includes a side door so the box can be cleaned out periodically. The bottom of the box is filled with four to six inches of sawdust or wood shavings to simulate the interior of a natural cavity. A six-inch wide strip of one-quarter-inch hardware cloth below the entrance hole on the inside gives the ducklings toe-holds for climbing out of the box. To reduce predation, nest boxes are placed on a metal post about four feet above the water in suitable habitat. If the water level fluctuates predictably, be sure to put the box above the high-water line. Predator guards (such as an inverted sheet metal cone) below the box discourage raccoons and snakes. Other cavity-nesters sometimes use nest boxes intended for woodies. Eastern screech owls, great-crested fly-catchers, starlings, squirrels, and

honeybees are just some of the likely tenants.

By March most female woodies have mates, and the search for nest sites begins. The hen initiates the search and selects the cavity. Within days, she begins laying eggs. A typical clutch of twelve eggs is cradled in the debris at the bottom of the cavity. Toward the end of the egg-laying cycle, the hen may pluck some of her own down feathers and add them to the nest.

After the hen incubates the eggs for about thirty days, they hatch, and the drake abandons the hen. Mom rears the brood alone. A few hours after the ducklings' first sunrise, the hen leaves the cavity and calls to the ducklings. They respond immediately by peeping and jumping up toward the cavity's hole. Clinging to the cavity wall (or to the hardware cloth installed in a nest box) with strong legs and claws, the ducklings gradually work their way up to the hole. Then, in what is truly a sight to behold, they jump to the ground or water below. Although natural cavities may be as high as sixty feet, the ducklings' small size and downy covering lets them land and bounce unharmed.

As soon as the entire brood is on the ground, it follows the hen back to the brood pond. Weak ducklings that can't make their way out of the cavity are left behind. Raccoons, squirrels, and snakes see that they don't go to waste. If the nest is some distance from the brood pond, the overland trip to water can be hazardous. The longer the journey, the greater the odds that a raccoon or snake will snatch some or all of the brood. That's why it's best to put nest boxes directly over the water. But even in the water, ducklings face constant danger from unseen predators below—snapping turtles, large fish, water snakes. Most of the older broods we saw on state lakes consisted of only three or four ducklings.

Those ducklings that survive grow rapidly on a diet of aquatic insects and invertebrates. By the time fall arrives, they are adult sized and have switched to adult foods—seeds and nuts of a variety of weeds and trees. Woodies eat acorns almost exclusively when they are available. At other times of the year mulberries, grapes, corn, and the seeds of buttonbush and bur reed round out their diet.

Despite the perils wood duck broods face each spring, they have stormed back from the brink of extinction, thanks largely to nest boxes. Just another bit of evidence that habitat—in this case, nesting habitat—is often the most critical factor to a species' survival.

R.J. Duke Lake

Size: 62 acres

RESTRICTIONS: nonpowered boats and electric motors only
MANAGING AGENCY: Ryerson Station State Park (1,164 acres)
LOCATION: near Wind Ridge, Greene County

This sentimental favorite is our home lake. Our girls had their first canoeing experience on R.J. Duke Lake, which lies just three miles east of the West Virginia border. Besides being a wonderful location for family outings, this lake stands alone as the only canoeable quiet water in Greene County. Greene County is rural ridge and valley country, much like the adjacent northern panhandle of West Virginia where we live. Wildlife abounds here.

Ryerson Station State Park gets its name from a fort built in 1792 to protect settlers from Indian raids. The park features a fifty-site campground on a ridge northeast of the lake. Ten miles of hiking trails allow exploration of the surrounding ridges and valleys. A boat rental concession rents rowboats and paddleboats on the lake's southwest corner, near the swimming pool, playground, and picnic areas. The Fish Commission stocks the lake with trout twice a year, and anglers also catch warm-water game fish and panfish.

From the dam at the north end, the lake curves gradually eastward into the marshy headwaters of North Fork. Except for the steeply wooded south shore, the lake is open and developed. But you will still encounter wildlife here, especially at the eastern end and in North Fork, which you can follow upstream for a half mile or more.

Duke Lake was the first lake we visited after agreeing to write this book. Our nine-year-old daughter, Nora, got caught up in the excitement of the project and wrote an extensive account of our trip in her journal. She did such a fine job that Scott printed it in his syndicated newspaper column. With that introduction, here's a nine-year-old's account of her first quiet water canoe experience.

> As soon as Dad parked the car, I opened the door and jumped out. Right away, Mom and Dad lifted the big red canoe off the roof. I was glad they did that in a hurry, because a seventeen-foot canoe looks pretty funny on top of a small van.
>
> My sister, Emma, and I put on our brightly colored sun hats, life jackets, and water shoes. This was the new canoe's first time

in the water, so we were all excited and a little nervous. We didn't want anyone to fall in on the first trip.

With Mom in the front, Dad in the back, and my sister and me in the middle, we were soon on our way. We paddled close to the shoreline, looking and listening for birds, dragonflies, and frogs. When we got to the end of the lake where a small stream flowed into it, we came to a wood duck nest box. Dad said the mother duck and her babies would have left the nest by now.

We continued to paddle upstream and soon noticed an even smaller stream flowing into the one we were in. It passed under the road through a large drainpipe. In the drainpipe was a mama black duck and her ten babies. We watched. It was amazing. The ducklings played follow-the-leader with their mom and stopped every few seconds to take a bite to eat.

Splish, splash, splish splash. A few minutes later we came upon a family of wood ducks. Dad said it might be the family from the nest box we had seen.

The wood ducks were the funniest and most exciting thing we saw all day. As soon as the mama saw us coming, she flew downstream and left the ducklings all alone. That seemed strange, but Dad said to be quiet and watch. The mother soon began calling to the ducklings. Immediately they flapped their little wings and ran toward her right on the top of the water. It was hilarious!

Suddenly, we noticed that one duckling had been left behind. We quietly moved the canoe to the edge of the stream. When the coast was clear, the duckling ran twice as fast as the others to reach its mother. When it went speeding by, we laughed so hard we almost tipped the boat.

After we calmed ourselves down, Mom and I switched places. Now I was in the front. We paddled slowly back toward the lake. When we passed the family of wood ducks, they disappeared into the tall grass at the edge of the water. At the drainpipe the black ducks were still eating.

When we stopped at the boat ramp, Dad told us all to get out of the canoe. He wanted to see how it handled as a one-man boat. As soon as we all got out of the canoe, the front end pointed up about two feet above the water. He looked ridiculous! I thought he was going to fall out. With the front end so far out of the water, he couldn't even steer.

It turned out he was just fooling around. He got on his knees and moved closer to the center of the canoe. That dropped the front end back into the water, and he handled the canoe just fine.

In the parking lot Dad smiled, pointed to his feet, and said, "Look." We all gasped. It was a killdeer nest. The eggs were really hard to see because they blended in with the gravel. Earlier, when we crossed the parking lot, one of the parent killdeer pretended to have a broken wing. It was trying to lure us away from the nest. Dad has seen lots of killdeer nests, so I guess he knew their trick.

Mom and Dad had told us that quiet water canoeing would be an adventure. They were right!

GETTING THERE: From Waynesburg, follow Route 21 west for 23 miles. Seven miles outside of Waynesburg Route 21 forks to the right. It's marked, so watch for it. Turn left at the park sign on S.R. 3022 and drive 1.4 miles to launch on the right. (You will drive past the dam and the park office.)

Dutch Fork Lake

Size: 91 acres

RESTRICTIONS: nonpowered boats and electric motors only
MANAGING AGENCY: Fish and Boat Commission
LOCATION: near Claysville, Washington County

We visited Dutch Fork Lake one early summer evening, about two hours before sunset. Cool breezes gently rippled the water's surface. Painted turtles sunned themselves on logs. Dragonflies lighted nearby, while the damselflies exploring our canoe kept our younger daughter occupied. The lazy dip of paddles, an occasional squawk of a green-backed heron, a green frog's "banjo string" call, the "plip" of a water snake dropping off of a rock and into the water—the lake's serenity and solitude seemed as immense as the blue sky above. It was the epitome of quiet water canoeing.

We hugged the shoreline, where all the action takes place. At the lake's north end, close to the dam, we paddled into a long, marshy cove reaching east. Through thick duckweed we drifted right up to a log blocking the end of the cove. We told the girls to watch for big, bulgy eyes. "Plop." A bullfrog jumped for cover—then another, and another. Emma, four, noticed a great blue heron flying above, heading, no doubt, to its roost many miles away.

Heading south again, away from the dam, we saw many rough-winged swallows. On the steep banks along some of the shoreline, we found holes where some of these birds were nesting. We tried "pishing and squeaking" (making birdlike sounds) to bring more birds closer into view. Many find these noises irresistible and come to investigate.

The shoreline of Dutch Fork Lake is largely wooded, except at the two launch sites. Here, the gently sloping banks are mowed and maintained for fishing access. The narrow lake stretches about 1.5 miles from north to south.

History buffs might be interested in the old cemetery just before the east-end access. Restored in 1956, this is the burial ground of the Jacob Miller family, early Pennsylvania pioneers and original proprietors of the area. Miller, who was born in Switzerland around 1722, was slain by Native Americans on March 31, 1782. The cemetery offers cool shade and solitude and a place to reflect. Nora said that it felt sacred, and she spent a long time just studying the gravestones and

Basking turtles are easily approached in a canoe, but they quietly slip into the water when the canoe gets too close.

imagining the people buried there, some only children when they died. A path from the east corner of the graveyard leads down to the waterfront along a small inlet.

GETTING THERE: From I-70, take the West Alexander exit (Exit 1) between Washington and Wheeling. Head east about 2 miles on U.S. 40 (Old National Road). Turn left at the sign for the lake onto S.R. 3001. Proceed about 200 yards to a larger wooden sign and turn right. This gravel road leads to the east launch site 1.5 miles away. To get to the west launch site, continue on S.R. 3001 for 1.4 miles past the east access turnoff. The parking lot and launch site are on the right and are clearly marked. This site is smaller and dirtier than the east access, but it serves the purpose.

Cross Creek Lake

Size: 258 acres

RESTRICTIONS: 10 H.P. limit

MANAGING AGENCY: Cross Creek County Park (3,300 acres)/Fish and Boat Commission

LOCATION: near Hickory, Washington County

HOURS: 6:00 A.M.–midnight, May–October; 8:00 A.M.–5:00 P.M., remainder of year

You may have already seen Cross Creek Lake, even if you've never been to Washington County. It was the setting for *The Dark Half,* a recent movie based on a Stephen King novel.

The perimeter of Cross Creek Lake makes it a fascinating place. The lake snakes about three miles long from its west-end dam to the marshy eastern fringes, reaching north and south with long fingers and protected coves. It takes the better part of a day to explore adequately these secluded areas, but the effort is well worth it. The area teems with waterfowl, especially during spring migrations. Even on a summer day you can expect to see families of ducks or Canada geese and great blue herons fishing the shallow shoreline. Beavers are active here, too. Most of the shoreline is wooded, but there are some fields and meadows that meet water's edge. Here you're likely to see deer during an early morning or evening outing.

This lake is fed by springs and small streams, many of which enter the lake through its numerous coves. The water is deep, ranging from about thirty feet along an old roadbed that runs along much of its length to sixty feet close to the dam.

Cross Creek Lake calls itself the sunfish capital of Pennsylvania. Fishermen pull an astonishing number of record-breaking sunfish from this lake—many more than from the next-best sunfish lake.

A covered bridge—one of twenty-six in this county—is located just east of the lake's easternmost reaches. Ask at the park office for directions.

The boat launch is located on the north shore in the center of the lake, right next to the parking lot, picnic pavilions, and park office at the main entrance. This launch features a special handicapped-accessible dock. A nearby private boat rental concession serves the park. Cross Creek Park requires a $5.00 annual launch fee for county residents; $7.50 for nonresidents.

Camping is not permitted in this park. For a list of local private campgrounds or more information, call Washington County Parks and Recreation at 412-228-6867 or Washington County Tourist Promotion at 800-531-4114.

GETTING THERE: From I-79, take the Bridgeville exit (Exit 11) and drive west on Route 50 for 17 miles. Turn left at sign for park entrance and drive 1 mile to parking lot and boat launch.

Raccoon Lake

Size: 101 acres

RESTRICTIONS: nonpowered boats and electric motors only
MANAGING AGENCY: Raccoon Creek State Park (7,323 acres)
LOCATION: near Frankfort Springs, Beaver County

Only twenty-five miles west of Pittsburgh, Raccoon Lake attracts many boating, fishing, and swimming enthusiasts. Yet even on a crowded summer day, we found this lake visually and biologically interesting. From its east-end dam, the lake jogs south a short way, then narrows and stretches west for close to a mile. A small cove just south of the dam contains the public launch and a boat rental concession.

We launched and headed west, toward the marshy headwaters of Traverse Creek. As we studied the distant marsh through binoculars, we just knew that exciting encounters awaited us. We hugged the dark and heavily wooded north shore. The girls asked if we'd see any bears as we glided past tall oaks and maples at water's edge. They seemed disappointed when we explained that a bear encounter was unlikely.

Past the swimming beach and a fishing jetty that juts well into the lake, we entered the marshy area. Nora spotted a mallard hen and ducklings. We sneaked past sedges and tiny "islands" of vegetation to catch a closer look. The hen was reluctant to take her babies out of the water, so she led them on a zigzag journey through the clumps of vegetation. They soon outmaneuvered us.

We entered Traverse Creek on the south side of the marsh and paddled upstream. If there is a current in this shallow creek, it was indiscernible to us. Rafts of organic debris gave the water a look and feel of stagnation. But here, between rocky cliffs on the south shore and lush wetlands on the north, we saw cedar waxwings, song sparrows, common yellowthroats, rough-winged swallows, eastern phoebes, turtles, and countless bluet damselflies and white-tailed skimmers (dragonflies). Our best discovery, however, was a phoebe nest clinging to the rocky cliff about thirty feet above the water. Phoebes build mud nests that can adhere to vertical surfaces. This one was completely in the open, yet so well camouflaged that only the bobbing heads of the nestlings gave it away. As we watched the nest, the adult phoebes sounded the alarm from trees nearby. They were clearly agitated. We watched for awhile, then left the spot in deference to their wishes.

As we headed back east toward the launch, the summer sun shined relentlessly, and we were all hot and uncomfortable. The girls didn't have to pester too hard to get us to stop off at the swimming beach. Boaters may moor just east of the beach. Nora and Emma took a leisurely swim while we stretched our legs on shore before the long paddle back.

As one of the largest state parks, Raccoon Creek provides many miles of hiking trails. A boat rental concession rents canoes and rowboats. A 176-site campground operates from mid-April to mid-December, and ten rental cabins are available. The park also features a swimming beach, picnic areas, and food concessions.

For more information, call the park office at 412-899-2200.

NEARBY: At the east end of the park, a wildflower reserve and visitor center feature impressive stands of native wildflowers along a five-mile network of hiking trails. Also interesting is the historic Frankfort Mineral Springs, located in the center of the park, south of the office and just off Route 18. This famous health spa attracted thousands of visitors during the 1800s.

GETTING THERE: The park is located just off U.S. 30, about 25 miles west of Pittsburgh. The boat launch is about 1.5 miles off of U.S. 30 at the lake's east end, near the dam. **Or** enter the park on Route 18, which bisects the park. The park office is located on the west side of Route 18. At the office, you can turn east and reach the launch via a park access road that runs south of the lake.

Eastern Phoebe

Most birds that migrate south for the winter wait until April or early May to return to their northern nesting grounds. By that time insects are emerging, and plants are leafing out. Eastern phoebes, however, always seem to rush the season. They are among the earliest migrants to return north each spring. I usually see at least one phoebe before the end of February. Phoebes like wooded rocky cliffs near water, so they are likely to be waiting to greet even the earliest spring quiet water canoeists.

Like so many birds, phoebes are common but probably unfamiliar to inexperienced birders. Lacking bright colors, they are often overlooked. However, anyone who listens to the sounds of nature certainly has heard their simple, self-identifying song—a raspy, oft-repeated "fee-bee." In fact, I usually hear the year's first phoebe before I see it.

Steep wooded embankments and ravines along seeps, springs, and streams are traditional phoebe habitat. They plaster their nests of mud, mosses, fine grasses, and animal hair on shelves under rocky ledges and overhangs. They also nest under bridges, in culverts, barns, sheds, and even on little-used porches. All they need is a small projec-

tion onto which they can anchor their nests.

When we moved into our house, it had been abandoned for some time. It stood empty, cellar door ajar. One of my first discoveries was a phoebe nest anchored to a basement joist. We let the nestlings fledge before building a new door. The next year the phoebes found the cellar tightly locked, so they nested in a shed only twenty yards away from the house. The following year they built a new nest in exactly the same spot, on a cross beam just above a window. Since then, a pair has nested on a beam right on our front porch. I'll admit the porch gets a little messy for the few weeks young are in the nest, but that seems a small price to enjoy such friendly neighbors.

In fact, phoebes are so familiar to my family that it's easy to forget their more traditional and natural habitat preferences. While paddling Raccoon Lake in Beaver County, however, I noticed a steep wooded cliff and explained to Nora and Emma that this was natural phoebe nesting habitat. No sooner were the words out of my mouth, than Linda said she thought she saw a nest. Linda's as sharp-eyed as they come, so we scanned the

area with our binoculars. Sure enough, we quickly spotted a phoebe nest jammed full of soon-to-fledge chicks tucked inconspicuously under an overhanging rock. We sat and watched for fifteen minutes as the parents brought a half-dozen meals to the hungry brood. Chalk another wild moment up to quiet water canoeing.

To the uninitiated, phoebes may seem rather nondescript. But their very drabness—together with their voice and a few behavioral characteristics—distinguishes them. Phoebes measure about seven inches long and are grayish black above and whitish below. While sitting on a favorite dead branch, power line, or length of barbed wire, phoebes repeatedly pump their tails up and down, a habit that permits experienced bird-watchers to identify phoebes by silhouette alone.

From these perches phoebes hunt flying insects in the distinctive way that characterizes members of the flycatcher family. A phoebe flies out from its perch, snatches a bee or wasp in midair, and then returns to the same perch. An attentive male can exercise this ritual for hours, alternately feeding himself, his mate, and his brood. During late-spring cold snaps when insects disappear, phoebes subsist on small fruits such as sumac and poison ivy berries.

Nesting begins soon after the birds arrive. Often a nest is completed by the third week in March. Egg laying is usually delayed, however, sometimes for as long as three weeks. Perhaps this insures that there will be an ample supply of insects when the eggs hatch. The female alone incubates the clutch of four or five white eggs for about fifteen days. The first brood hatches in late April or early May. A second brood usually follows in June.

There are many traditional signs of spring, but most are unreliable. Weather is absolutely unpredictable, and robins, contrary to popular belief, remain in many parts of Pennsylvania all winter long. But phoebes seem to respect our calendar. They return just as we are growing weary of winter. Sometimes snow still covers the ground. Get to know these friendly little fly-catchers, and you'll learn, as we have, that phoebes are among nature's truest harbingers of spring.

Yellow Creek Lake
Size: 720 acres

RESTRICTIONS: 10 H.P. limit
MANAGING AGENCY: Yellow Creek State Park (2,981 acres)
LOCATION: near Penn Run, Indiana County

On a map, Yellow Creek Lake looks like some kind of prehistoric animal. Our daughter Nora was the first one to notice it. She pointed out how the main body of the lake runs east to west, with a long "neck" jutting northwest toward the dam and three "legs" extending southward. There's even a "tail" at the east end that pokes north. And like prehistoric lakes we imagine, this one is shallow in many places and thick with submerged vegetation.

According to local birders, Yellow Creek Lake ranks as one of the best spots in western Pennsylvania to see migrating waterfowl. A waterfowl observatory looks out over Grampap's and Gramma's coves to the south. Warblers frequent the shoreline in this area and also on the northeast shore.

Two areas best serve canoeists.

The first is a small launch site located at the east end, near the park office. From here, we headed east, hugging the southern, marshy shoreline on our way to the headwaters of Yellow Creek. This is a good place to observe migrating waterfowl in the spring and fall. But duck hunters hunt here in the fall, so plan your visit accordingly.

The lake's eastern end becomes quite shallow, and we were forced to get out of the canoe twice to push free of the muck. We eventually made it to Yellow Creek, which flows clear, cold, and several feet deep. The Fish Commission stocks this creek with trout, and we saw several small brook trout. We paddled under the Route 422 bridge, then had to turn around because the water became too shallow.

Just south of the creek is Laurel Run Cove. Water lilies have pretty much overtaken this cove. But we sat for awhile just inside its mouth and observed white-tailed skimmers—the large dragonflies with white abdomens and dark wing bands. Actually, only the males have the white "tails." The female's abdomen is dark with small yellow spots, and her wings have small, dark patches as opposed to bands.

White-tailed skimmers belong to the most common family of dragonflies in North America—the Libellulidae. We've seen white-tailed skimmers on virtually every lake we've ever visited. They typically fly along the water's edge or perch on shoreline vegetation. In Laurel Run Cove, we watched a female depositing eggs. She'd touch her abdomen to the water, fly up and around in a loop, and touch the water again in a different spot. Over and over she repeated the movement, attaching her eggs to the submerged vegetation.

The second good quiet water spot is the southwest portion of the lake. The access here is on the east shore of Grampap's Cove. From here, you can head west to explore the extensive marshy area known as Gramma's Cove, a birding hot spot, or head into the wooded northwest neck, toward the dam.

The park's most developed area is along the south shore. Here are located the swimming beach, picnic area, food concession, and a boat rental concession that rents canoes, rowboats, pontoons, sailboats, and motorboats. Camping is not permitted on park lands, but there is a private campground on Campground Road, near Grampap's Cove, and others close by.

For more information, call the park office at 412-463-3850.

GETTING THERE: From the junction of U.S. 422 and Route 119, south of Indiana, travel east on Route 422 for 10.4 miles to the park's main entrance, then turn right onto Route 259, and travel about 1 mile to the east end launch. To get to Grampap's Cove at the south end, travel south on Route 259 2 miles past the east-end launch, then turn right onto Campground Road. Drive 1.4 miles to the launch. (Halfway to the launch, the paved road turns to gravel.)

Glendale Lake

Size: 1,600 acres

RESTRICTIONS: 10 H.P. limit
MANAGING AGENCY: Prince Gallitzin State Park (6,249 acres)
LOCATION: near Frugality, Cambria County

Evening approached, and the sun was slipping down behind the trees. It had been a long day on Glendale Lake, yet we couldn't resist the lure of one more cove to explore. We launched on the south shore of Wyerough Branch and paddled west, under a bridge, toward the headwaters of Wyerough Run. We passed several fly fishermen working the two little coves on the north shore. Hemlocks line the shore here. The state tree of Pennsylvania, hemlocks once abounded in this region before they fell to the woodcutter's ax a century or two ago. Among other things, hemlocks provided tannic acid used in the tanning of buffalo hides.

A narrow channel cut through the marshy plants and shrubs at the headwaters of Wyerough Run. We entered the channel, but our exploration was cut short by a beaver dam several hundred yards upstream. We heard the beaver before we saw it—that characteristic tail slap on water. We caught a brief glimpse and it was gone. Light was fading fast, so we opted to return to the launch rather than hang around for more beaver watching.

But what was that song? We heard a musical trill, each note on the same pitch. Then we saw the bird, perched in the buttonbush about ten feet away. We froze. Chestnut-colored back, rusty head, black markings behind the eyes—a swamp sparrow! It posed for minutes as we paused to admire. When it finally flushed, we could easily see its tail pumping in flight. The swamp sparrow nests in the tall, dense vegetation found along swamps, streams, and marshes. The headwaters of Wyerough Run would certainly qualify.

A little farther downstream we paused for Scott to do his famous screech owl call. When we are bird watching, Scott uses this tremulous whistle to call birds into view. Most songbirds fear the predacious, nocturnal screech owl and will mob it when it calls during the day. Imagine our surprise when a real screech owl poked its head out of a wood duck box nearby. Screech owls, which are cavity nesters, have been known to use wood duck boxes, but we had never witnessed it.

Working our way back to the launch, we saw a rock bass in the clear, shallow water and another gelatinous bryozoan (see page 70 for detailed explanation). All in all, it was a productive ninety minutes on the water.

Situated on the Allegheny plateau, Glendale Lake encompasses twenty-six miles of shoreline. From its dam at the north end, the main body of the lake stretches south for more than four miles, ending at Mud Lick. Three large coves extend westward from the main body, including Wyerough. Another, major branch, called the Slate Lick Branch, breaks away at the east side of the dam and extends south for about three miles, roughly paralleling the main part of the lake. Glancing at a map, the entire lake looks a little like a wishbone.

The Slate Lick Branch is one of three areas we'd recommend to canoeists. However, plan to visit on a weekday either before July 4 or after Labor Day. During the peak summer season, this fascinating area hosts too many pontoon boats for our taste. Long and narrow, this branch will require a full day to explore, so pack a lunch. The southern tip, at the headwaters of Slate Lick Run, is choked with water lilies, but a channel cuts through the vegetation. There are no launches (or roads) along the Slate Lick Branch, but you can put in at Beaver Dam launch, just south of the dam on the lake's west shore. Launching here requires a paddle across deep, open waters that are often choppy, so be careful.

Another area we heartily recommend is the Wyerough, the northernmost of three arms extending westward from the lake's main body. This area, described above, can be reached from the pontoon mooring area launch.

The third area ripe for canoeists is the lake's southern tip, which includes Mud Lick and Killbuck coves. These coves can be reached from the Killbuck launch on the west shore. They both extend into rich, marshy areas with irregular shorelines and lots to see. We saw two does in this area, each with twin fawns. There were great blue and green-backed herons here, too.

Each of the recommended areas would be best visited sometime other than the peak summer season. Please note, however, that each of these areas is open to hunting, so avoid these areas during hunting season or visit on a Sunday.

The large Prince Gallitzin State Park features many facilities for visitors. Named for the Russian prince and ordained priest who served the area's settlers during the early 1800s, the park contains 437 campsites open from mid-April through mid-December. Ten rental cabins are available year-round. The park also features a swimming beach, food concession, eight public launch sites, boat rentals, and numerous picnic tables and pavilions.

For more information, call the park office at 814-674-1000 or the park campground at 814-674-1007.

GETTING THERE: From the intersection of Route 219 and Route 422, north of Johnstown, take Route 219 north for 9.3 miles. Turn right at the stoplight in Carollton onto East Caroll Street. Go 4.5 miles to Route 36 in Patton. Turn right and take Route 36 south 0.6 mile. Bear left onto L.R. 11084 and drive 5.2 miles to park office. To get to the launches and areas we recommend, turn north (left) onto L.R. 11052 just before (west of) L.R. 11084. This road leads to the campsites, dam, and main part of the park.

Northwest Region

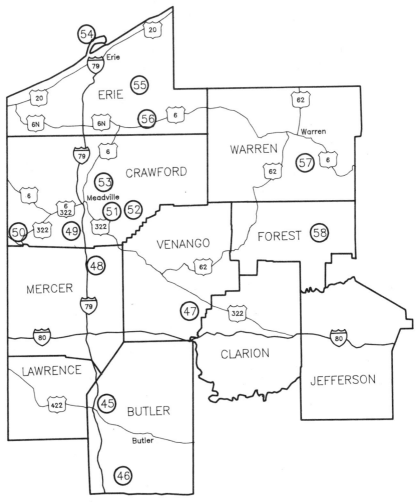

45. Lake Arthur
46. Glade Wildlife Lake
47. Kahle Lake
48. Lake Wilhelm
49. Conneaut Marsh
50. Pymatuning Lake
51. Tamarack Lake
52. Pool 9

53. Woodcock Creek Lake
54. Presque Isle Lagoons
55. Lake Pleasant
56. Union City Reservoir
57. Chapman Lake
58. Beaver Meadows Lake

Northwestern Pennsylvania is (or was) glacier country. Glaciers receding 10,000 years ago deposited the soils and scraped out the depressions and rolling hills so characteristic of this region. Glacial lakes and moraines are constant reminders of the area's icy past.

The region is fairly well populated, with a major population center in Erie, and smaller ones in Meadville and Warren. But most of the region's eastern half is rugged and isolated, with towns few and far between. Here, and in the north-central region, it's easy to understand that woodlands cover two-thirds of Pennsylvania.

Scenic U.S. Route 6, the Army of the Republic Highway, passes many interesting sights in the northwest, including the world-famous Kinzua Bridge. At 301 feet high, it was the world's highest railroad bridge when it was built in 1882. Today it's part of a state park and can still be traversed—by foot or by special railroad car.

A large portion of the half-million-acre Allegheny National Forest is located in the northwest, as well as the Allegheny River and the Kinzua Dam, which creates the huge Allegheny Reservoir.

In the heart of the northwest, the world's first drilled oil well was located in Venango County in 1859. A replica of this well can be seen at the Drake Well Museum.

The 12,000-acre Allegheny Reservoir can be canoed, but limit yourself to the extreme upper reaches of the reservoir's fingers unless you want to contend with motorboats and choppy, windy waters. Located primarily in Warren County, the reservoir extends east into McKean County, and north into New York. It encompasses 91 miles of shoreline.

Lake Arthur

Size: 3,225 acres

RESTRICTIONS: 10 H.P. limit
MANAGING AGENCY: Moraine State Park (15,848 acres)
LOCATION: near Prospect, Butler County

Lake Arthur is a must-see. It is a reclaimed ancient glacial lake. In fact, the entire park, mostly wooded or marshy, has been reclaimed from coal mines, coal strippings, and oil and gas wells that covered the area for nearly eighty years—a fact we found amazing, given the area's striking beauty. The main body of the lake extends east/west, with three long arms branching south, two branching north, and countless coves and fingers. This configuration produces a fascinating but sometimes confusing body of water, so before canoeing be sure to stop by the park office for a map.

Of eleven launch sites, we recommend five on the lake's more remote and biologically significant areas. Three are close together on the lake's east end—each accessible from Route 528, which runs north/south through the park. The first is Church launch on Shannon Run, just south of the Route 528 bridge. The second is just north of the Route 528 bridge. Both provide easy access to Shannon and Swamp runs and Muddy Creek. Each of these long arms reaches into marshes and is heavily used by waterfowl and other birds. Loons are reportedly common here and elsewhere on the lake during spring and fall migration. There is also a wildlife propagation area (off-limits to boaters) at the end of Swamp Run. Six osprey were released at Lake Arthur in 1993—the first ever in this area. The Game Commission is planning to release more of these magnificent fish-eating raptors over the next three or four years, according to Butler County's Land Management Group Supervisor, Ned Weston.

Be sure to check out the cliff and barn swallow colonies under the Route 528 bridge. The nests and birds can be seen from the water, or get an even closer look from the launch parking area directly under the bridge. These colonial nesters are fun to watch—and tragic, too. When we last visited, a gruesome sight greeted us. At three separate nests, dead swallows dangled in the breeze, tangled in monofilament line. We looked closer and were shocked to find that at least half of the dozens of mud nests had tangles of monofilament hanging from them. Apparently, the swallows use the carelessly discarded line as nesting material. Later, at the park office, we were dismayed to discover that no special efforts were being made to educate or even warn fishermen of the dangers to wildlife caused by their carelessness.

Improper disposal of monofilament line is a recurring problem across the state. Because it does not biodegrade, monofilament line is a serious litter problem and health hazard to fish and wildlife. At least part of the blame for this lies with the state. We saw no recycling boxes or signs explaining the dangers of fishing line anywhere. Anglers must learn to pocket used line and dispose of it properly in trash containers. At the very least, they should learn to cut balls of line into small pieces that cannot entangle wildlife. In the meantime, canoeists can spread the word and pick up any line they find while paddling the commonwealth.

The third eastern launch site is farther north on Route 528, a little more than a mile north of the bridge. The launch puts you about halfway up the Muddy Creek arm.

The fourth launch site we recommend is located on Big Run at the southernmost tip of the lake, adjacent to the Regional Forestry Office off old Route 422. Again, shallow, marshy coves make this an ideal wildlife-watching area. To get there, take U.S. 422 and exit on Route 528. Head north for several hundred yards, then turn east (left) onto old Route 422.

A fifth launch site, on Bear Run, provides access to the lake's westernmost point. Here, the marshy end of the run terminates in a cattail pond. Look (or rather, listen) for Virginia and Sora rails. These secretive marsh dwellers are difficult to see, so they rank high on many birders' "want" list. You can reach this launch by taking Exit 28 off I-79, heading west, then making an immediate north turn (left) onto Badger Hill Run and driving about 1.2 miles. Or, approaching from the east, take U.S. 422 to Pleasant Valley Road. Head west 0.8 mile, turn right (west) on PA 488, and proceed 1.1 miles to Badger Hill Road.

We largely ignored the highly developed north shore and Pleasant Valley day-use area along the south shore. Here you'll find six more launches, boat and bike rental concessions, marinas, swimming beaches, a restaurant, picnic pavilions, group camping sites, and cabins. Sailing is a popular activity on the lake, and races and regattas occur all summer long. Unfortunately, there is no individual family camping in this park. We found a private campground on Badger Hill Road, just before the launch on Bear Run. The park office can suggest other private campgrounds nearby.

For more information, call the park office at 412-368-8811.

NEARBY: Be sure to visit the nearby Jenning's Environmental Education Center, north of Lake Arthur on Route 528. This area is ecologically significant as the home of the endangered massasauga rattlesnake and a remnant population of blazing star (*Liatris spicata*). On this small remnant patch of glacially formed prairie, blazing star, a member of the sunflower family, blooms in early August. Each individual plant consists of a tall single stalk upon which a spike of purple flowers adds another touch of color to the palette of summer wildflowers.

GETTING THERE: From I-79, drive east on Route 422 for 2.7 miles to Pleasant Valley Road. The south shore office is just north of this intersection and well marked with signs. The north shore turnoff is just 0.3 mile east of I-79. Head north and follow the park signs.

Litter

A dead cliff swallow dangling from its nest in a tangle of monofilament line is a grim reminder of the price wildlife pays when anglers litter used fishing line.

The sight sickened me. The lifeless body of an adult cliff swallow dangled in the breeze beneath its globular mud nest, suspended from a tangle of fishing line. Just above the swinging body another adult, perhaps its mate, fed the chicks inside the nest. I scanned the other nests in the small swallow colony and discovered fishing line from at least half of them.

Fishermen enjoy respect in the world of conservation and outdoor recreation. You see them everywhere—at secluded lakes, in state parks, and even along urban riverfronts. Often the scene is family oriented. Moms and dads introduce the kids to rods, reels, bobbers, and live bait. Whether catching one or a dozen, the thrill of hooking and landing even a sunfish never dulls. Fishing seems somehow above the fray of controversy.

At least, that's how I've always perceived it. Until recently. What I've observed while canoeing lakes all across the state disturbs me. There are slob fishermen. Lots of them. Though my observations are limited to Pennsylvania, I suspect the problem transcends geographical boundaries.

At the very least, some fishermen are serious litterbugs. It's easy to assign blame because the trash gives them away. Too many toss their Styrofoam bait containers and used monofilament line in the water or along the shoreline. Some might argue that littering is a minor problem. Eyesores are relatively easy and cheap to clean up. Unfortunately, fishing-related litter can have much more far-reaching consequences. Styrofoam is not biodegradable. If it's there today, it will be there tomorrow, next week, and next year.

Improperly discarded fishing line poses an even greater threat to wildlife. It, too, persists long after it's been discarded. The fishing tackle industry has promoted the proper disposal and recycling of monofilament line for years. Ducks, geese, and herons entangled in fishing line, especially when such scenes show up on local television news broadcasts, are bad for business. That's why we see recycling bins for fishing line at many bait and tackle shops. And though these bins get used, my recent observations suggest they are being ignored by far too many.

The Route 528 bridge that spans Lake Arthur in western Pennsylvania's Moraine State Park shelters the small colony of barn and cliff swallows where I found the birds entangled in fishing line. By the time I finished an informal survey, my concern that fishing line might be a hazardous nesting material was justified. I found one adult barn swallow and two cliff swallows "hanging" in the breeze below their nests. Each had gotten hopelessly tangled in the line and strangled when they tried to leave the nest. The image made a lasting impression on my whole family. Who knows how many birds die this way each year?

The good news is that the solution to this serious problem is simple. Anglers must responsibly dispose of all their used line. *Never* throw used line in the water or on the shore. Just stuff it in your pocket. Throw it away or put it in a recycling bin at the end of the day. State parks and other fishing areas could help by placing informational posters and line recycling bins at every boat launch and parking area. Pennsylvania's state parks make trash cans available, and most have recycling bins for glass, metal, and plastic. But we've seen none for monofilament line.

The Fish Commission doesn't even attempt to make litter control a priority. Few of the lakes it managed had trash cans, and those that did hid them in the rest rooms, where they remained unseen except by those who couldn't resist the urge to use a pit or portable toilet. The Fish Commission's only attempt at litter control at most of the sites we visited were prominent signs announcing that litter was illegal. Signs and warnings may seem a wonderful bureaucratic solution to the problem, but in reality no one really "sees" them. It seems that a state agency that spends millions of tax dollars buying land, stocking lakes, and mowing grass could invest just a bit in litter control.

No fisherman wants to hurt birds or other wildlife. Most simply don't realize the potential dangers of monofilament line. A little education and a little peer pressure can help a lot. If trash cans or recycling bins are not available, just stick used line in your pocket until you get home.

Then cut through the loops with a scissors and dispose of it permanently. The fishermen I've mentioned this to have all been appalled by the problem and immediately volunteered to do their part.

It is up to anglers to police their own ranks. State agencies can regulate, and the fishing tackle industry can educate, but as Bill Wohl, Public Relations Manager for Stren Fishing Lines, told me recently, "The ultimate responsibility lies with the individual angler." By taking this responsibility seriously, anglers can retain their coveted status as respected conservationists.

Glade Wildlife Lake

Size: 400 acres

RESTRICTIONS: nonpowered boats only
MANAGING AGENCY: Game Commission
LOCATION: near Montieau, Butler County

Glade Wildlife Lake is a veritable "duck factory," judging from the dozens and dozens of wood duck boxes and Canada goose nesting platforms located all over the lake. Managed by the state Game Commission and surrounded by state game lands, this lake includes several wildlife propagation areas. Much of the lake is thus off-limits to canoes, but there's still a lot to see and paddle through. From its dam, the lake extends southeast about a mile.

For ten months of the year, the entire northwestern two-thirds of the lake is closed as a wildlife propagation area off limits to boaters. This is to give waterfowl a refuge from hunting and boating pressures. The area is open to boats from June 15 to August 31. These dates correspond with the period when bank fishing is prohibited.

The southeastern shallow end, opposite the dam, is open to boaters year-round, except for another propagation area at the far end of the lake. This propagation area, closed from March through August, protects a very active bald eagle nest in a large tree at the lake's southeast end. According to Ned Weston, Land Management Group Supervisor for Butler and Lawrence counties, this nest produced three young eagles in 1991, another three in 1992, and one in 1993. He notes that the late-March snowstorm of 1993 was probably responsible for killing other eggs that year. Bald eagles in Canada and Alaska average two chicks per nest, but Weston speculates that the abundance of carp in Glades Wildlife Lake gives these eagles a reliable food source.

From April to about August 15, the lake's water level is lowered two feet, cutting the surface area in half, to about 200 acres. Subtract from that the areas tied up in wildlife propagation, and you have about fifty acres left for canoeing during the late spring. Even at that, the area is worth paddling, if only to admire the families of young ducks and geese and catch a glimpse, through binoculars, of the nesting bald eagles. When you paddle through the shallow south end, though, remember to keep your distance from nesting ducks and geese. One nesting season, two-thirds of the birds incubating eggs abandoned their nests after being repeatedly chased off by curious "lookers," Weston claims. "It's a modern day phenomenon that we love our wildlife to death," he adds. We'd recommend a July or August visit to Glade Wildlife Lake. By this time, most young ducks and geese are out of the nest, and the large and scenic northwest section of the lake near the dam is open to boaters.

We launched from the west shore near the south end. The "launch" is an extremely shallow, muddy channel cut through a goose-infested marshland. The channel leads to the southern portion of the lake. It was so shallow in some spots that we used our paddles to pole and push our way through the muck. Finally we reached deeper water and headed southeast. This shallow end is a maze of nesting structures, marshy islands, emergent stumps, floating logs, and water lilies. It looked a little like an Ansel Adams landscape. Scott took lots of photographs. At the far edge of this area stands a tall, dead tree, and in this tree is lodged a bald eagle nest. We saw no evidence of the birds, but the huge nest itself was a magnificent sight.

GETTING THERE: From I-80, take Exit 4 and head south on Route 308 for 11.5 miles. Turn left onto Tinker Road, and travel 1.1 miles on dirt road to the launch. *Or* from Butler, head north on Route 8 for about 2 miles to Route 308. Travel north for 11.5 miles, then turn right (east) onto Tinker Road and proceed 1.1 miles to launch.

Kahle Lake

Size: 250 acres

RESTRICTIONS: nonpowered boats and electric motors only
MANAGING AGENCY: Fish and Boat Commission
LOCATION: near Mariasville, Venango County

At first glance, Kahle Lake doesn't look like much more than a good place to fish. Surrounded by farmland and an occasional woodlot, the lake lies in fairly well developed farm country. But looks can be deceiving. For us, Kahle Lake turned out to be a wildlife bonanza.

From its dam at the west end, the lake extends east. A large cove reaches northeast, and another smaller one is located on the north shore in the middle of the lake. The clean, clear waters are filled with *Elodea* (submerged vegetation), and the shoreline is fringed with cattails, sedges, and small willows. A few water lilies grow in the northeast cove.

As we explored the large cove, we flushed a large bird from the woodlot on the north shore. It circled overhead, and we had plenty of time to observe with our binoculars. It was an immature bald eagle! Later we learned that local fishermen had heard of eagles in this area.

On the cove's mudflats we saw many killdeer. And great blue and green-backed herons fished the shallow waters. At least three separate wood duck families worked the cove's western edge. Two of the families disappeared into the sedges as we paddled near, but one group tried to outswim us. We raced briefly, then the ducks veered away toward the opposite shore.

Heading west toward the dam we noticed another large bird soaring overhead. This one was all white, with a black "cap" and a large, reddish bill. We quickly identified it as a Caspian tern, although we were surprised to find one in midsummer. Bird range maps show Caspian terns nesting north of Lake Erie, so perhaps we saw a solitary individual that had lost its mate. As we watched it, the tern soared for awhile, its broad wings giving it a gull-like appearance. Eventually it lighted on the water and floated, and we continued on our way into a small cove on the north shore.

A flotilla of Canada geese greeted us as we entered the cove. They left in a hurry, and we spent the rest of our visit fish watching in the cove's clear waters.

Later, as we were leaving the area, we noticed an unusual note tacked onto the Fish Commission's rules and regulations board. Someone reported seeing two loon chicks on June 1 and was asking others who had seen the chicks more recently to contact her. Again, an unusual occurrence this far south.

GETTING THERE: From I-80, take Exit 6 and head north on Route 38 for 3.4 miles. Turn right onto a dirt road, drive 1 mile, bear left at Y in the road, and proceed another 0.2 mile to launch on the lake's south shore.

Lake Wilhelm

Size: 1,860 acres

RESTRICTIONS: 10 H.P. limit
MANAGING AGENCY: Maurice K. Goddard State Park (2,856 acres)
LOCATION: near New Lebanon, Mercer County

Lake Wilhelm stretches more than eight miles northwest from its dam to its marshy outer reaches. More than three miles of the lake's western end are surrounded by state game lands and open only to nonpowered boats. This 420-acre portion is by far the most interesting and least used. The remainder of the lake is located within the state park. Here, motorboats of up to 10 H.P. are permitted. There are eight launch sites on the lake, including three on the state game lands. We recommend the two westernmost launches, one on either side of a propagation area located right in the center of the state game lands portion of the lake. The propagation area is closed to boaters, so it's impossible to paddle the entire length of this western 420 acres. The portions you can reach, however, are definitely worth the effort.

Western Lake Wilhelm is essentially a flooded forest, with scores of snags—standing dead trees—jutting from the water. These snags provide excellent perching for kingfishers, herons, eastern kingbirds, and nest sites for woodpeckers and tree swallows.

Shortly after putting in at the westernmost launch, we found three kingbird nests tucked into the broken tops of three different snags. Each contained the characteristic heavily speckled eggs. Kingbirds frequently nest in trees or bushes over water. They are aggressive, feisty birds and fiercely protect their nests against predators.

This area is also dotted with wood duck boxes and artificial nesting platforms for geese. Our girls loved the young, downy goslings we saw everywhere on an early June morning. Geese grazed and swam all over this area. We also saw a half dozen great blue herons. A muskrat startled us as we approached a floating log. It had been swimming alongside a log and turned abruptly with a splash when it saw us.

The floating and submerged logs form a real obstacle course in this part of the lake. Several times we grounded on one and had to carefully back up to free ourselves. Too often, novice canoeists try to push sideways or ahead to unlodge, exposing themselves to the very likely possibility of tipping over. There's nothing more unstable than a high-

Standing dead trees teem with life at the western end of Lake Wilhelm, a haven for cavity-nesters such as woodpeckers, bluebirds, and wood ducks.

centered canoe. Also adding to the challenge of canoeing this section were the thick beds of water lilies and duckweed.

You can explore the lake east of the propagation area from a launch near the S.R. 1018 bridge. We'd also recommend the launch along the south shore at the eastern edge of the state game lands. This launch lies just east of a log boom, which precludes access to the west. But you can head east and pass under the I-79 bridge to the marshy part of the lake located on the western edge of the state park. This interesting area can also be reached from Launch Area 3, near the park office.

GETTING THERE: From I-79, take Exit 34 and head west on U.S. 358 for 0.3 mile. Turn right at sign for park and proceed 1.1 miles. Turn right at stop sign onto S.R. 1009 at sign for park and go 2.3 miles to Launch Area 3, just past the bridge.

To get to state game lands portion of the lake, proceed west from the park office on S.R. 1014 for 1.6 miles, then turn left on S.R. 1018. Travel 1.2 miles and make a sharp right turn, just past the bridge. This launch is located just east of the propagation area.

Another launch west of the propagation area can be reached by continuing on S.R. 101 another 1.2 miles past S.R. 1018. Turn left onto Cemetery Road and drive 0.5 mile to this westernmost launch site.

To get to the third launch on state game lands, head west on Creek Road (south of lake) and drive 1.1 miles on dirt road to launch.

Conneaut Marsh (Geneva Swamp)

Size: 5,619 acres

RESTRICTIONS: no motors
MANAGING AGENCY: Game Commission
LOCATION: near Geneva, Crawford County

Conneaut Marsh teems with wildlife and plant life. This marsh, the largest in the state, is also called Geneva Swamp. Actually, the area includes both marsh and swamp. A marsh is an area of herbaceous vegetation and standing water with no perceptible current, although it is not self-contained, like a natural lake. Water and nutrients enter and leave the system. Water lilies, cattails, low shrubs, grasses, and sedges characterize the vegetation. A swamp, on the other hand, is a wooded wetland. Here, you find willows, sycamore, sweet gum, dogwood, alders, buttonbush, and other woody plants.

Marshes and swamps are disappearing at an alarming rate in Pennsylvania, as elsewhere. Often, these biologically productive wetlands are dammed (in both senses) and converted into lakes. Wetlands represent only 2 percent of the state's land area, but they support one-third of the state's breeding birds.

Conneaut Lake, a natural glacial lake to the northwest, nourishes Conneaut Marsh and forms the channel canoeists can follow through thick mats of smartweed, pickerelweed, water lilies, and cattails. Classified as a kettle lake and formed thousands of years ago by a melting ice block, the 938-acre Conneaut Lake today is a popular motorboating, waterskiing, and recreational spot.

Conneaut Marsh, by contrast, hosts few visitors. It is our favorite quiet water location. Accessible only by canoe or kayak, the marsh promises a change of scenery and a new wildlife encounter with each paddle stroke. During a recent visit, our girls remained actively involved in wildlife watching even after four hours in the canoe!

The marsh can be explored in two sections: east of I-79 and west of I-79. The eastern portion, which drains into French Creek, eventually passes through woodland and farmland. Canoeists can expect to portage over or around many downed trees, and the route is especially challenging during times of low water. Also, a trip through this eastern portion requires a shuttle from the takeout point back to the put-in point.

Nora counts the eggs in an eastern kingbird nest at Conneaut Marsh.

We recommend the western end. The launch site is the Geneva Dike area. From here, you can canoe for about 5.5 miles to Mud Pike, depending on water levels. As you head northwest, the open marsh gradually transforms into wooded swamp. Yellow water lilies, cattails, and buttonbush give way first to willows, then eventually to other hardwoods.

Shortly after we launched, we heard slight splashing in the buttonbushes. We sat tight. Several minutes later, a deer poked its head through the brush, knee-deep in water. When it spotted us, it turned and waded away. We heard it splashing through the vegetation for many minutes. Later, as we approached the swamp to the northwest, we paddled past a raccoon on a log under a willow tree. It never even flinched as we passed closely.

Washed-out dams and logjams indicate beavers in this area, and bobcats and opossums also reportedly inhabit the swamp. Huge carp splash in the weeds, sucking up vegetation. Green frogs and bullfrogs twang and bellow, then plop into the water. Dragonflies and damselflies abound, as well as other, more annoying flying insects. (Be prepared!)

But it's the bird life that's really exciting. Bald eagles nest successfully in the area. We saw two immatures soaring overhead. Wood ducks, black ducks, mallards, and Canada geese are common. We also saw marsh wrens, bank swallows, great-crested flycatchers, goldfinches, common yellowthroats, yellow warblers, robins, and several bickering kingfishers putting on quite a show. We found an eastern kingbird nest in a low shrub right in the middle of the marsh. The girls almost tipped the canoe trying to get a peek into the nest. They managed a good, long look at the three darkly speckled eggs.

Though marsh wrens are declining rapidly in Pennsylvania, a visit to Conneaut Marsh in May or June almost guarantees seeing many. They are abundant in the cattail prairies that dominate the marsh. Their loud, bubbly sound is easy to recognize and, once learned, it remains in the mind as one of the marsh's defining sounds. Look for their distinctive globular nests tucked among the cattail stems.

Red-winged blackbirds were undoubtedly the most common species at Conneaut. But we startled a fair number of great blue herons, too, prompting them to spread their massive wings and slowly lift up off the water to land a short distance away. Green-backed herons are common here, too. And we saw three American bitterns in flight.

Emma warms up after an early morning adventure on Conneaut Marsh.

But the "best" bird was one we only heard: a Virginia rail. Singing in a dense cattail stand, it wasn't spooked by our clumsy efforts to catch a glimpse. Rails are extremely difficult to see. They don't flush when frightened, they just walk deeper into dense vegetation. Determined birders will find Virginia, king, and sora rails at Conneaut.

As with quiet waters everywhere, conditions vary according to season at Conneaut Marsh. In late September, water levels are low, but migrating waterfowl flood the area. Spring and early summer visitors find better canoeing conditions, but more insects. Avoid visiting during waterfowl hunting season from October to December, except on Sundays, when hunting is prohibited.

For more information on either the western end or eastern end of Conneaut Marsh, call the Western Pennsylvania Conservancy at 412-288-2777.

GETTING THERE: From I-79, you can reach the Geneva Dike and the marsh's launch by taking Exit 35 and heading west on Route 285. Cross over Route 19 and continue on Route 285 for 2.6 miles, heading toward Geneva. Turn right at the second Geneva intersection (*before* the green sign listing Conneaut Lake and Linesville mileage), and proceed 1.2 miles to a small bridge. Park in the wide gravel Y of the road. You can launch your canoe near the small bridge.

Rails

Sooner or later anyone who canoes marshes and cattail-fringed lakes will encounter rails. These secretive and unfamiliar birds live amid the dense vegetation that surrounds lakes, swamps, and marshes. Perhaps it's the difficulty of finding these birds and the challenge of flushing them that appeal to birders and hunters who seek rails. That's why I seek them out with my binoculars. I've never met a rail hunter, so I don't know what motivates them. I have read, however, that in the bayous of Louisiana, rails are considered a delicacy. (But then, in the bayous of Louisiana, anything that moves is considered a delicacy.)

Of the nine species of U.S. rails, I've seen only six. And three of those are gimmees. Walk the Anhinga Trail in the Everglades and purple gallinules, common moorhens (formerly called common gallinules), and American coots are sure bets. In Pennsylvania, moorhens and coots can occasionally be seen in larger marshes that include some open water, especially during migration. They may be walking in the mud along the water's edge or swimming like ducks. But a quick glimpse of the moorhens' and coots' chicken-like bill readily distinguishes them from other waterfowl. Both moorhens and coots nest in the state, but neither can be considered a common breeder.

Of all the rails, coots are the most common and widespread. They are perhaps best known as the mascot of Corporal Klinger's beloved Toledo Mud Hens on television's "M.A.S.H." Their dark gray bodies and white bills make them easy to recognize. And while swimming they often dive to feed on submerged vegetation. Fleshy lobes on their toes give coots the paddle power they need for diving.

The remaining six species of rails are elusive inhabitants of the marsh. Three (sora, king, and Virginia) have been confirmed to nest in the state, though kings are extremely rare and found only in a few isolated wetlands around the state. Clapper rails prefer coastal salt marshes, and yellow and black rails might be seen as occasional migrants.

Cryptically colored and streaked with earth-tone markings, true rails rarely leave the protective cover of dense marsh vegetation. Their bodies are compressed from side to side, making it easier for them to pass through the grasses, reeds, and rushes that characterize most wetlands. And their long, skinny toes enable them to walk on soft, muddy bottoms.

Because rails are both uncommon and elusive, they can be difficult to see. Their population has declined thanks to habitat destruction and water pollution. Rails are just one more reason conservationists fight to protect and conserve the nation's remaining wetlands. It's an old refrain, but wetlands support myriad forms of life.

Conneaut Marsh in Crawford County is rail heaven. This 5,619-acre wetland provides abundant cover for Virginia rails, soras, moorhens, and coots. While paddling west of I-79 in June we head the unmistakable metallic, "Ki-dik, ki-dik, ki-dik" of a Virginia rail. We listened for twenty minutes, and I even slogged around the cattails for awhile, but we never did see the bird. It was a typical rail hunt.

To see rails, paddle through wetlands and marshes slowly and quietly. The best times to see them are early and late in the day. Scan the marsh's edge with binoculars or, better yet, a spotting scope (a telescope for birders). Watch for movement along the line where the water meets the vegetation.

Virginia rails are about nine inches long, have long bills, and rich chestnut-colored wing patches. Soras are about an inch smaller, but they have a short, thick, yellow bill. Both have distinctive calls that are better heard than described. But once experienced, these calls will forever be etched in the listener's mind as sounds of the marsh.

Pymatuning Reservoir
Size: 16,500 acres

RESTRICTIONS: 10 H.P. limit
MANAGING AGENCY: Pymatuning State Park (21,122 acres)
LOCATION: near Linesville, Crawford County

Millions of people each year visit Pymatuning Reservoir, the state's largest body of water after Lake Erie. This monstrous lake straddles the Pennsylvania/Ohio border, with three-quarters of its water lying on the Pennsylvania side. The area was once a huge swampy wetlands. One can only imagine the waterfowl and other wildlife it supported. But in 1868 the state's general assembly initiated an effort to "reclaim" the swamp, and by 1934 a dam on Shenango River was completed. Today, such actions would be illegal.

The area has a fascinating prehistory, too. Long ago, early Americans known as the "Mound Builders" occupied this whole section of Pennsylvania. During colonial times, the Iroquois lived here and bestowed the name "Pymatuning," which means "The Crooked-Mouthed Man's Dwelling Place." Apparently, the name referred to the deceitful dealings of the Erie Indians, who made their home here before the Iroquois occupation. After the Indian Treaty of 1785, homesteaders from New York and Connecticut arrived and settled Pymatuning.

From the dam at the south end, the lake curves north more than eight miles, then jogs suddenly southeastward for another mile and a half to the Route 18 bridge. East of the bridge and off-limits to canoeists and other boaters is another 2,500 acres of water that are part of a wildlife refuge.

Development crowds the lake's southern end, and launches and boat moorings litter the eastern shore. The most appropriate areas for canoeists in this heavily used lake are along the northern tip and the north shore west of the wildlife refuge. Three good-sized islands— Clark, Harris, and Whaley islands—are located just off the north shore and are accessible by three different launches: Alcatraz, Wilson, and Linesville. The shoreline near these launches and along most of the north shore is marshy.

We recommend the westernmost Wilson launch, at the lake's northern tip. This launch is easy to find at the end of Wilson Road, just off U.S. 6, yet it doesn't have the shoreline development and nearby

RJM

houses that the other two northern launches have. Also, this launch puts you in a good position to explore the many coves, lagoons, and inlets characterizing the northern tip—or to head due south to Clark Island, largest of the northern islands. A deeply recessed inlet on the east shore nearly cuts the island in two.

Wind and waves will definitely be factors to consider on a lake of this size. We've been faced with rough, choppy water each time we've visited Pymatuning, so our outings have been briefer and more confined to shoreline than they ordinarily would have been. But even if you visit Pymatuning on a windy day, there's still a lot to see and do, especially south of Linesville and U.S. 6 along Lines Hart's Road and the spillway that bisects the lake's eastern branch.

For example, plan to visit the fish hatchery in the wildlife refuge portion of the lake. This hatchery, managed by the state's Fish Commission, features a wonderful exhibit of mounted fish and information about different species. But we most enjoyed the two-story tank filled with real fish. You can peer into the open top of this tank, or look through glass windows at the bottom to see huge catfish, bass, sunfish, gar, and more. We also saw Fish Commission employees working with the fingerlings growing in huge tanks.

Also along Lines Hart's Road in the wildlife refuge portion of the lake is the waterfowl museum on Ford Island, less than a half mile south of the fish hatchery. This museum is owned and operated by the Pennsylvania Game Commission. Plan to spend at least an hour here examining the waterfowl and wildlife exhibits, hiking the quarter-mile shoreline trail, and looking for bald eagles and other bird life at the observation area just outside the building. We found a mature bald eagle perched on a log just off the shoreline. With our binoculars we had a wonderful look at its bright white head, black body, and huge, yellow talons.

The third and most popular attraction along Lines Hart's Road as it crosses the lake's east branch is the fish feeding station right at the spillway. Here, hordes of people buy stale bread to feed to the multitudes of carp that blanket the shoreline and pier area. We saw signs and T-shirts in Linesville advertising this as "The place where ducks walk on the fish." And that's exactly what happens. The sucking, writhing carp are so thick that the ducks and Canada geese literally walk right over them to snatch bits of bread for themselves. Personally, we were revolted by the whole spectacle. The water in that area is filthy and fouled, plastic bread wrappers litter the shoreline, and people are interacting with wildlife in a totally inappropriate way. The feeding station really draws tourists, though.

Pymatuning State Park features 807 family camping sites and a number of rental cabins. The park makes a great headquarters for canoeists who want to explore the many great lakes and marshes of Crawford County. There are also four swimming beaches, picnic areas, hiking trails, boat rentals, and food concessions.

For more information, call the park office at 216-293-6329. **Note:** The park office is located at the southern tip of the lake, far removed from the northern tip we recommend for canoeists. We suggest you call the office ahead of time and ask that a park map be mailed to you.

NEARBY: Crawford County features a lot of quiet water. Think about making Pymatuning State Park your base of operations for visits to Conneaut Marsh, Woodcock Creek Lake, the Erie National Wildlife Refuge, or Tamarack Lake.

GETTING THERE: From U.S. 6 in Linesville, travel about 1.7 miles west to Wilson Road. Turn left and travel just a short distance on dirt road to Wilson Launch. This is the westernmost launch at the lake's north end—the launch that puts you in the best position to explore the marshy and interestingly configured northern tip. From here you can also head south to explore Clark Island or west into some large, marshy coves.

To visit the fish hatchery, waterfowl museum, or fish feeding at the spillway, head south on Lines Hart's Road from its intersection with U.S. 6 in Linesville. *Or* from I-79 west of Meadville, take U.S. 6 west for about 2.5 miles to Linesville. Proceed as directed above.

Tamarack Lake

Size: 562 acres

RESTRICTIONS: nonpowered boats and electric motors only
MANAGING AGENCY: Fish Commission
LOCATION: near Meadville, Crawford County

Southeast of Meadville, Tamarack Lake stretches northwest from its dam for about 3.5 long, narrow miles. Even though it lies close to a large population center, the lake remains undeveloped and largely unspoiled. Its shoreline is wooded on all but the southwestern edge, where most of the boat launching and bank fishing occurs.

Marshy fringes and little coves all along the eastern shore invite the canoeist for a closer look. We found a family of Canada geese, blankets of blooming white water lilies, and about a zillion small sunfish clearly visible in the pondweed below. In fact, we almost tipped the canoe here because Nora and Emma were so intent on fish watching that we couldn't convince them to sit still.

We'd recommend launching from the south end at the second launch site. This gives easy access to the marshy southeastern edge, and from there, you can explore the more interesting and untamed eastern shoreline.

GETTING THERE: At the intersection of Route 322 and Route 173, southeast of Meadville, near Cochranton, go west on Route 322 for 0.8 mile to blinking traffic light, then turn right (north) at sign for Tamarack Lake onto S.R. 2007. Proceed 4.8 miles to Freyermuth Road and turn left (there's a lake sign at intersection). Go 0.5 mile to Tamarack Drive, then turn right and go 0.3 mile to first launch at dam and south end of the lake. *Or* from Meadville, head east on Chestnut Street past the David Mead Inn and turn right onto Grove Street. Go 0.2 mile (past two stoplights) and turn left at stop sign onto Williamson Road. Drive another 1.7 miles, then turn left on Tamarack Road and go 2.6 miles to first launch at the north end of the lake.

Altogether, there are six launch sites along the west shore and another one on the east shore at the lake's north end.

Pool 9
Size: 130 acres

RESTRICTIONS: no motors

MANAGING AGENCY: Erie National Wildlife Refuge (Sugar Lake Division)

LOCATION: near Guys Mills, Crawford County

Erie National Wildlife Refuge is only one of two (the John Heinz National Wildlife Refuge at Tinicum in the southeast corner of the state is the other) national refuges located in Pennsylvania. It exists primarily to provide ducks and other waterfowl with nesting, feeding, brooding, and resting habitat. The refuge's 5,137-acre Sugar Lake Division includes 2,500 acres of wetlands—marshes, swamps, beaver floodings, creeks, and artificial impoundments. Canoeists may use 130 of those acres on "Pool 9." (Leave it to a federal bureaucracy to come up with such a creative name for such a wonderful place.)

Pool 9 is not for the faint of heart. Depending on water levels, you can expect to portage your canoe about 100 yards from the cement dike to water's edge, then walk through thick, foul-smelling pond muck until the water's deep enough to float the canoe. Our girls hated this muck, so we ended up portaging them as well. Once you're in the canoe and on your way, insects and submerged logs will challenge and annoy you.

But diehards will be well rewarded. The refuge attracts 236 bird species, including 112 that nest. Wood ducks are common nesters in this area. Other common nesters include hooded mergansers, mallards, blue-winged teal, Canada geese, great blue herons, red-tailed hawks, and American kestrels.

During migration—March to early April and September to November—other waterfowl join these summer residents. Refuge employees report regular sightings of black ducks, golden-eye, pintail, green-winged teal, scaup, American wigeon, bufflehead, and ring-necked ducks. When you are paddling the pond, don't forget to look skyward occasionally. Bald eagles and osprey fish here and can often be seen circling overhead. We thought we saw an immature eagle from a distance, but we weren't able to make a positive identification.

Pool 9 is fairly shallow, so seasonal fluctuations in water level will determine how much of the 130 acres you can cover. The mostly

Pool 9 at Erie National Wildlife Refuge offers great early morning birding in May and June.

wooded shoreline features a narrow marshy fringe of cattails, smartweed, bulrushes, and sedges. Red-winged blackbirds are among the most common nesters in this marshy fringe.

GETTING THERE: From Meadville, take Route 27 east for almost 9.5 miles until you come to an intersection with S.R. 2013 and a large sign for the refuge. Continue on Route 27 another 0.5 mile, then turn right (south) onto Boland Road. Drive 1 mile on this dirt road to a parking area on the right. Turn into this parking area and proceed west through a gate and another 0.5 mile to the Pool 9 dam. You can park right along the concrete dam.

The refuge headquarters and visitor center are located about 3 miles north of the Pool 9 parking area. To get there, drive back out to the intersection of Route 27 and S.R. 2013 (at refuge sign) and travel north on S.R. 2013 for 2.2 miles. Turn right (east) on Route 198 and proceed 0.8 mile to headquarters access road on right.

Woodcock Creek Lake

Size: 500 acres

RESTRICTIONS: 10 H.P. limit
MANAGING AGENCY: Army Corps of Engineers
LOCATION: near Meadville, Crawford County

Only about five miles northeast of Meadville, Woodcock Creek Lake offers fascinating opportunities for exploration and nature watching. Even though motorboats of up to 10 HP are permitted here, they generally stay west of the Route 1003 bridge. That's okay with us, because we prefer the lake's eastern end. State game lands surround much of the east end. This area boasts a great variety of wildlife. Small islands and peninsulas of marshy vegetation dot the northern shore. The water here is shallow. Beware of the old roadbed running east to west in this area. During late summer you may ground your canoe here.

Cattails, sedges, rushes, willows, some sycamores, and other wetland vegetation shelter creatures such as the great blue and green-backed herons, turtles, frogs, red-winged blackbirds, kingfishers, and wood ducks we saw. As we made our way northeastward into a marshy cove ringed with wood duck nesting structures, we noticed the water rippling in front of the canoe. A muskrat swam to shore and disappeared into a hole in the muddy bank. The banks are riddled with such holes, suggesting a healthy muskrat population. Wild irises grow profusely here. Most are blue, but we also saw some with white or lavender flowers. The water is remarkably clear in this lake; with our binoculars we could watch minnows and painted turtles negotiating the submerged vegetation.

From the cove in the extreme northeast corner, we retraced our route 100 yards or so to cut between a peninsula and an island. Then we continued northward into Woodcock Creek. The beautiful tree-lined creek remains canoeable for some distance. We paddled several hundred yards, then turned around. Heading back to the launch, we hugged the south shore, admiring the hemlocks prominent among the steeply wooded banks. Fallen trees partially submerged add to the beauty and wildlife potential of this shoreline.

A word of advice about the east-end launch site: There is no ramp, just a steeply sloping bank reinforced with concrete. It's a little tricky to negotiate, so scout around for the best spot. We entered directly below the center of the parking lot. You'll have to portage your canoe anywhere from about forty feet to 100 yards or more, depending upon where you park. Also, the rest rooms were locked and the ground generally unkempt when we visited in early June. But the chance to explore this exciting lake is well worth these minor inconveniences. This east end launch lies just east of the bridge. We paddled under the bridge looking for nesting swallows but found none. From here you could continue west into more open waters and the county park portion of the lake. Campsites are available at Colonel Crawford County Park at the lake's west end. For information, call the park at 814-336-1151.

NEARBY: A scenic walkway across the breast of the dam extends for more than one-half mile. It affords a wonderful view of the lake's west end and Colonel Crawford County Park on the south shore. You can reach this walkway from Route 198, which parallels the north shore. Also, plan to visit Bossard Nature Center, which is directly across from the scenic walkway on the other side of Route 198.

GETTING THERE: From U.S. 6 in Meadville, take Park Avenue exit (U.S. 19) and drive about eight blocks to Chestnut Street. Turn right and drive east for 0.4 mile to Grove Street. Turn left and go 0.3 mile to State Street, then turn right and go 0.1 mile to S.R. 27 at stoplight. Make a quick left onto S.R. 77 (Clark Street). Drive 1 mile, then bear left onto Dickson Road and go 4 miles to launch access road on the right, just before the bridge.

A second access is located at Colonel Crawford County Park, 0.3 mile before the bridge on the opposite side of the road. *Or* from I-79, take Exit 37 and head east on S.R. 198 for 8.2 miles. Follow the road signs closely, as Route 198 twists and turns and passes through Saegertown. Just past the dam at the lake's west end, turn right on S.R. 1003 and drive 0.4 mile to the launch, located just across the bridge, on the left. This is the marshy and "wilder" side of the lake—the area we prefer. To get closer to the dam and the lake's west side, travel another 0.3 mile past the bridge to Colonel Crawford County Park. Camping and other facilities are available here. For information, call the County Courthouse at 814-336-1151 or the County Park at 814-724-6879 (Memorial Day through Labor Day).

Presque Isle Lagoons
Size: several miles of interconnected lagoons

RESTRICTIONS: nonpowered boats and electric motors only
MANAGING AGENCY: Presque Isle State Park
LOCATION: near Erie, Erie County

On Presque Isle State Park, a small peninsula that juts into Lake Erie, a series of interconnected ponds or lagoons provides a fantastic quiet water canoeing adventure. In May and September this area is one of the nation's top birding hot spots. And the lagoon system represents a living textbook on ecological succession—from pond to marshland to wooded swamp and everything in between.

Presque Isle is a seven-mile-long, 3,200-acre sand spit peninsula in Lake Erie. The entire peninsula has been designated a National Natural Landmark due to the diversity of habitats found here—sand dunes, sand plains, ponds, marshes, lagoons, swamps, and forests. This peninsula was formed by prevailing westerly winds, waves, and currents acting on glacial sands. Over many years, separate ponds formed inside the peninsula. In the 1930s, dredging linked many of the ponds. Water now flows continuously from Misery Bay west to Marina Lake. This dredging has had some negative ecological consequences, such as the invasion of non-native aquatic plants. But for canoeists, it provides one of the best outings in the state.

The only inland access to the lagoon system is the launch on Grave Yard Pond. As its name suggests, this pond has a colorful history. During the winter of 1813–1814, a cholera outbreak occurred among Commodore Oliver Perry's sailors stationed in Misery Bay. To dispose of the victims' bodies, the men cut holes in the ice of a nearby pond and gave their shipmates a watery grave.

The pond is a much nicer place today as the starting point for the lagoon tour. The round-trip covers four miles or more, depending upon how far you paddle into some of the connecting ponds. Be sure to take a park map along. The various coves and branches of the ponds pose a navigational challenge, and sometimes the main channel is difficult to see beyond the water lilies, cattails, smartweed, and other vegetation.

We launched and headed north through Grave Yard Pond, then west into the first connecting channel. As we rounded a bend into Big Pond, our eyes were drawn south to the Erie skyline. The distant

Pristine woods and wetlands make Presque Isle one of the country's best birding spots in spring and fall.

skyscrapers look curiously out of place with lily pads and cattails in the foreground. Our attention riveted by the strange sight, we paddled south into Big Pond and missed the channel we should have taken. (It cuts due west.) Fortunately, the thick water lily beds soon alerted us that we had missed the main channel, and we quickly retraced our route.

Tree swallows abound in the lagoon system. They nest in the snags lining the route. Red-headed woodpeckers also are common. They like lots of open space with large, scattered trees. The marshes ringed by large deciduous trees apparently meet their needs. We saw two. One just flew in front of our canoe, disappearing into the cottonwoods. But the other one entertained us a bit as it clung to a dead tree at water's edge. Wood chips flew as it drilled into the snag. Even without binoculars we could all see its distinctive red head; white chest, rump, and wing patches; and black back. The girls were transfixed. When a rowboat rounded the bend, the bird gave an alarm call and flew away.

All along the route we saw many green-backed and great blue herons, kingfishers, painted turtles, red-winged blackbirds, mallards, and several species of dragonflies and damselflies. Bald eagles occasionally feed here, too, although we didn't see any. The dense stands of reeds and cattails provide excellent nest sites for American bitterns, sora, and marsh wrens. (You are more likely to hear these three species than see them.) And Presque Isle is just one of a few places in Pennsylvania where prothonotary warblers nest. Also watch for beaver lodges along the way. We saw two.

We found the plant life equally fascinating. Pickerelweed, smartweed, cattails, wild irises, yellow and white water lilies, yellow water buttercups, rushes, submerged pondweed, swamp rose, highbush blueberry, winterberry, buttonbush, and silky dogwood grow in the marshy zones. Where the marsh gives way to swamp, you can see red maple, green ash, pin oak, and the tall eastern cottonwood.

Plan to take a picnic lunch when you explore the lagoons. There are five lovely picnic spots along the route, each with a small dock, picnic table, and trash can. Some people fish from these picnic docks. Fishing is permitted along the entire lagoon system, and fishermen catch bass, pike, sunfish, crappies, and bluegills.

In three leisurely hours we paddled west all the way to Marina Drive Bridge and back again to the Grave Yard Pond launch. You can proceed past the bridge and through a 200-yard channel into Marina Lake.

From Marina Lake it's possible to head east into Presque Isle Bay and eventually into Misery Bay and under the Misery Bay Bridge into Grave Yard Pond, thus completing a giant circle. But we strongly

Erie's skyline reminds paddlers in the Presque Isle lagoons that civilization is not too far away.

caution you against attempting this loop. Strong winds, high waves, and large motorboats can make the open bay waters and even Marina Lake a treacherous place for canoes and other small boats. Instead, simply retrace your route from Marina Drive Bridge back to Grave Yard Pond, enjoying the scenery and wildlife you may have missed the first time. The currents and winds even within the lagoon system will give you a good workout.

Time your Presque Isle Lagoon canoe outing for the warmer months. Bird migrations peak in May and September, so these times would be excellent. The summer months showcase blooming water lilies, wild irises, swamp rose, and other flowering plants.

A boat livery on Grave Yard Pond next to the public launch rents canoes from May through September and offers free, guided pontoon boat tours of the lagoon system. There are three afternoon tours daily. Reservations are required.

Seven miles of hiking trails wind through Presque Isle State Park and showcase various stages of ecological succession. The visitor's center offers interpretive exhibits of park flora, fauna, and habitats.

There is no camping permitted on Presque Isle, but the park office can suggest local private campgrounds.

For more information, call the park office at 814-871-4251.

GETTING THERE: From I-79, take Exit 43 and proceed west on 26th Street for 1 mile. Turn right onto Route 832 (Peninsula Drive) and go about 1 mile to the park entrance. Proceed another 5.5 miles to Misery Bay Bridge. The Grave Yard Pond launch and parking area are just north of the bridge.

Lake Pleasant

Size: 60 acres

RESTRICTIONS: nonpowered and electric motors only
MANAGING AGENCY: Fish Commission access, but lake is privately owned
LOCATION: near Wattsburg, Erie County

Glaciers formed much of northwestern Pennsylvania, leaving deep depressions in the earth where natural lakes formed in their wake. Such was the case with Lake Pleasant, one of only seventy-six natural lakes in the entire state. This big, round lake lies among rolling farm fields and small woodlots. During the last Ice Age, as the glacier receded, it scooped out an impression in the gravelly soil. Rainwater and the melting glacier collected there, forming the lake. The surrounding hillsides, known as glacial moraines, are characterized by the gravelly, sandy soil left by the same receding glacier.

While its geological history is probably its most interesting feature, Lake Pleasant offers a pleasant quiet water experience. We leisurely paddled its perimeter in about an hour. Marshy vegetation rings the shoreline except on the east end, where the shoulder of Lake Pleasant Road meets water's edge. A lot of bank fishing occurs here. On the summer evening we visited the lake, there were also a fair number of fishermen in boats. A local man told us that most people fish the lake for walleye, pike, and bass.

The only other natural glacial lake we recommend for quiet water canoeing is Upper Woods Pond in Wayne County. Canadohta Lake and Conneaut Lake, both in Crawford County, also are large, natural glacial lakes, but heavy lakeside development and use render these sites virtually useless for quiet water canoeing.

NEARBY: Combine Union City Reservoir, about ten miles to the southeast, with Lake Pleasant for an interesting day of canoeing.

GETTING THERE: From the intersection of U.S. 6 and Route 8 in Union City (40 miles west of Warren), head north on Route 8 for 4.5 miles. Turn left on Arbuckle Road and drive 3.8 miles, then turn left at lake sign (which is part of the Methodist Church sign) onto Lake Pleasant Road. Drive 0.5 mile to lake. There is no formal launch site, but the road skirts the lake's east shore and you can easily launch a canoe from anywhere along this east side.

Union City Reservoir
Size: 60 acres

RESTRICTIONS: cartop boats and canoes only, no motors
MANAGING AGENCY: Union City
LOCATION: Union City, Erie County

According to local anglers, Union City Reservoir supports an excellent population of muskie and bass. One man claimed that a canoeist he knew hooked a muskie he couldn't land because the fish was so large, it kept pulling the canoe all over the reservoir.

Tall fishing tales aside, the reservoir really is a fun site. With its dam at the west end, the lake is shaped like a Y, with the bottom of the Y reaching north, one arm reaching south, and the other reaching west. The shoreline is undeveloped and mostly wooded. We saw a huge beaver lodge on the east shore, opposite the dam. And there appears to be lots of beaver activity, particularly in the north branch. In the evenings, canoeists and anglers hear a lot of tail slapping and see the bubble trails made by beavers swimming underwater.

This is a small lake that can easily be canoed in an hour, unless you spend time to watch the beavers, as we did. Any small lake near a town experiences a lot of fishing pressure, and this one is no different. The summer evening we visited, there were at least ten people fishing from the bank—but no one in a boat. Canoeists would probably have more solitude during a spring or fall visit.

Try combining a visit to Union City Reservoir with a trip to nearby Lake Pleasant, a natural glacial lake (see page 170).

GETTING THERE: From the intersection of U.S. 6 and Route 8 in Union City, head east on U.S. 6 for two miles, then turn left at a small, obscure lake sign and drive 0.6 mile on dirt road to the lake.

Chapman Lake

Size: 68 acres

RESTRICTIONS: nonpowered boats and electric motors only
MANAGING AGENCY: Chapman State Park (805 acres)
LOCATION: near Clarendon, Warren County

Due south of Warren, Chapman Lake offers a fine canoeing and wildlife-watching experience within a short drive of a major town. State game lands and the Allegheny National Forest surround most of the park. The lake stretches from its dam southwest to the mouth of Tionesta Creek (West Branch).

Several interesting coves and fingers at the creek's headwaters attract wildlife and give canoeists a challenging route to explore. This area is marshy and heavily channeled by beavers. Beaver "paths" are everywhere. The main channel snakes its way around tiny islands and mudflats, where shorebirds such as spotted sandpipers and killdeer probe for invertebrates. Many wood duck boxes have been erected here. And, indeed, the coves and crannies formed by the headwaters are great refuges for waterfowl.

Encountering this family group of common mergansers at Chapman Lake proved that wood ducks aren't Pennsylvania's only cavity-nesting ducks.

One of our best wildlife encounters occurred in this area, when we rounded a bend and came face-to-face with a flock of twenty-three common mergansers. The group probably represented two or even three family groups—hens and their nearly full-grown ducklings. They were as startled as we were, and they "raced" through the channel and out into the open lake. They soon calmed down, though, and we followed them for awhile. They seemed to almost get used to our canoe, and we were able to shoot lots of photographs.

Like wood ducks, common mergansers nest in cavities. But they are too large to use wood duck boxes. Park office employees told us later that plans are under way for erecting special merganser boxes.

Heading southwest again, we followed the lake's main channel through the marsh to where Tionesta Creek enters the lake on its east side. Even in summer the channel is generally deep enough for a canoe to travel almost a mile. This is a wonderful trip, if for no other reason than to study beaver ecology. Little side channels created by beavers cut through the creek banks, and we saw many beaver burrows. Beavers have built several lodges along the creek, as well as a large lodge at the mouth of the creek. Partially gnawed trees, wood debris, and paths through the shoreline vegetation give further evidence of the large rodents. Beavers do most of their "work" between sunset and sunrise, so if you hope to actually see them, plan your trips accordingly.

The upper reaches of Chapman Lake is a great place to see and study beavers.

In addition to canoeing, recreational opportunities abound at Chapman State Park. There are twelve miles of hiking trails inside the park and unlimited hiking in the 517,000 acres of Allegheny National Forest and state game lands surrounding the park. Chapman is the starting point for many people planning extensive backpacking trips. An eighty-three-site campground with pit toilets is open from April through December. And a boat rental concession rents canoes, rowboats, and paddleboats.

For more information, call the park office at 814-723-5030.

NEARBY: The Struthers Library Theatre in nearby Warren features summer stock and professional-quality theater. Performances are held Thursday through Sunday evenings. The beautifully ornate theater, listed on the National Register of Historic Places, was built in 1883.

GETTING THERE: From U.S. 6 in Warren at Ludlow Street (intersection of Route 62 and U.S. 6), travel south for 7 miles. Turn west (right) at stoplight in Clarendon onto Chapman Dam Road. Proceed 5.1 miles to the park office and drive another 0.7 mile to launch on west shore.

White-tailed Deer

No matter how often I see a white-tailed deer, and I see some almost every day, they grab my attention. At home, I stop what I'm doing and watch. On the road, I pull over for a quick study. And any time one appears at the edge of a lake or bounds through a marsh, we stop and enjoy.

I admire their vigilance. Any unexpected movement or sound puts them on alert. Heads jerk. Ears cock. Feet stamp the earth. The leader snorts defiantly, then flees, waving its white flag in warning, not surrender, to the rest of the herd.

Often it's the big-racked bucks that draw the most attention. And perhaps that's as it should be. After all, their antlers (not horns) are intended to attract attention—from does and other bucks. White-tailed bucks, like most male members of the deer family, wear antlers as a sign of social and sexual status. The larger the rack, the more dominant the buck. When sizing each other up during the rut (breeding season), bucks often meet, rack to rack, in ritualistic sparring matches. Only rarely do these contests escalate into serious fights where one or both bucks risk injury.

Misconceptions about "antlers" and "horns" are com-mon. The terms are not synony-mous. Antlers grow and shed annually, not unlike leaves on deciduous trees. Members of the cattle, goat, and sheep family wear horns their entire lives. Antlers are made of solid bone. Horns consist of an inner bony core covered by an outer layer of tough fingernail-like material. Antlers begin to grow in early spring. Their final size depends on a combination of factors: the buck's age, its health, its diet, and its genetic background. A set of horns grows throughout the life of the animal wearing them.

Developing antlers are engorged with blood vessels and nerves and covered with hairy skin called "velvet." The soft, sensitive velvet is easily injured. Injuries to velvet can cause deformed antlers. The bucks we saw during our summer of quiet water research were "in velvet." Antlers continue to grow throughout the summer. Then the bone hardens, and the velvet dries and sloughs off. After the rut, in January or February, hor-monal changes cause the base of the antler to weaken, and the rack falls off. In late March, increasing day length triggers a hormonal process that renews the whole cycle.

When I try to analyze my fas-cination with deer and antlers, I come up with a number of possible explanations. It's the only large wild animal I see regularly; perhaps size and my interest level are directly proportional. Maybe it's because they are so darn beautiful. Or maybe it's the memory of a delicious venison tenderloin that flickers in the cobwebs of my mind.

Perhaps I envy how deer thrive amidst the havoc we've wreaked upon the planet. They bring a sense of wildness and adventure into an otherwise tame and predictable world. A glimpse of a deer in a marsh makes it seem all the more wild. Yet sometimes they conjure up quite contrary images, too. Like late one Christmas night, when I hit one near my mother's Montgomery County home.

In less than the blink of an eye, a doe appeared out of nowhere and mangled $1,000 worth of fender and glass. Deer/car collisions are not unusual; in 1992 alone, Pennsylvanians killed more than 42,500 deer on state highways. Insurance claims total tens of millions of dollars annually, and sometimes human lives are lost. And have you ever met a farmer or rural landowner who did *not* complain of deer damage to crops, shrubs, and gardens?

Beautiful. Graceful. Vigilant. Delicious. Destructive. How is it that one animal can evoke such a range of descriptions? To understand this enigma we need only examine recent history and the white-tail's reproductive prowess.

The exploding deer population that destroys crops, gardens, cars, and human lives is more a by-product of human history than the result of game management. Deer thrive in secondgrowth forest and edge habitat, not mature forests. The forests of Pennsylvania, and much of the East for that matter, are still recovering from extensive logging that occurred from the late 1800s through the 1930s. And what is suburbia, where many of us live, but vast chunks of recovering second growth? This, combined with urban prohibitions on hunting, helps explain why deer populations are so high in areas of dense human populations.

Eastern forests' long-term ecological recovery from unregulated logging in decades past provides abundant food and cover for deer. As long as foresters maximize timber harvest by cutting trees before they mature, second-growth forests will persist. And so will unnaturally high populations of deer.

If hunters don't kill enough deer each year to keep deer populations in check, deer damage increases. Consider Gettysburg National Military Park, where hunting is not permitted. In some parts of the park, deer numbered as many as 170 per square mile last year. The density recom-

mended by the Game Commission for similar farm/woodland habitat is 20 deer per square mile. Hal Greenlee, the park's resource management specialist, says, "At these high densities, deer eat 75 percent of the new growth in the woods. Without regeneration, these woodlands will eventually disappear." Habitat destruction is the ultimate legacy of an unmanaged deer herd.

Furthermore, only a small fraction of available deer habitat is actually managed. Game Commission biologists monitor the statewide status of the deer herd. Based on the estimated number of deer, summer food supply, and the severity of the previous winter, they set harvest goals to maintain what they feel is an ideal herd size. These goals take into account the natural history of the animal as well as human concerns such as deer/car collisions and damage to crops, gardens, and backyard trees and shrubs.

What managers can't control, however, is the distribution of the harvest across the state. In Pennsylvania, for example, the Game Commission owns and manages 1.3 million acres of state game lands. Throw in 2.5 million acres of state and national forest land, and you've got about 4 million acres of public hunting land. That's a lot of land. But it's still less than 15 percent of Pennsylvania's total area. Most of the rest is privately owned. And on more and more of that private land, hunting is not permitted.

On one hand, the Game Commission monitors the deer herd closely and regulates its harvest; on the other it has little control over most of the land where deer live. The primary management tool is regulating the number of licenses sold per county and then hoping hunters achieve a predetermined harvest. So while it may superficially appear that state game managers control the deer population, their impact is less than one might expect (or hope). Successful deer management, as measured by meeting harvest goals, relies as much on the willingness of private landowners to permit hunting and the weather on opening day (when most deer are shot) as it does upon science.

Compounding all these management problems is the white-tail's enormous reproductive potential. At first it may seem unimpressive. A typical doe bears just two fawns each year. But up to a third of female fawns breed in their first fall, and many does live five to seven years. Ten to fourteen fawns over the course of a lifetime is many more than are needed to maintain a stable population. Even when predation, disease, and other mortality factors are considered, a deer herd in good habitat grows 20 to 40 percent per year. A herd growing at 20 percent doubles in four years; a 40 percent growth rate doubles a herd in two years.

The deer's mating system complicates the situation. Dominant males breed with many females, so fewer bucks than does are required to maintain a stable or even growing population. Thus, managers can justify a long buck season and short doe season, and still the herd grows. Hunters' quest for bucks, their unwillingness to shoot does, managers' reluctance to expand the doe harvest, and the white-tail's naturally high reproductive potential combine to keep annual deer kills at conservative levels.

Though white-tails are unquestionably beautiful and graceful animals, understanding their natural history clarifies why their populations must be managed. Regulated hunting is the simplest, most cost-effective, and most efficient way to control exploding deer populations, minimize deer damage complaints, and reduce the annual roadkill toll. The best part from the public's perspective is that deer hunters not only eagerly provide this valuable service, they pay for the privilege as well.

Beaver Meadows Lake

Size: 50 acres

RESTRICTIONS: nonpowered boats and electric motors only
MANAGING AGENCY: Allegheny National Forest
LOCATION: near Marienville, Forest County

Like many of the lakes in northern Pennsylvania, Beaver Meadows Lake was constructed in the 1930s by the Civilian Conservation Corps. And like many of the northwestern lakes, this one is a converted wetland. Years ago, before people understood the biological and ecological importance of marshes, swamps, bogs, and other wetlands, they viewed such areas as wastelands and converted them to croplands or dammed them to form lakes.

From its dam at the west end, Beaver Meadows Lake extends due east to shallow headwaters and a series of tiny "islands" of cut-grass. Cut-grass, with its serrated edges that "cut" when touched, rings almost the entire shoreline, while conifers border the shores. In the hills behind the conifers we could see the hardwood forests heavily damaged by the recent elm spanworm invasion. The white bodies of the adult moths littered the forest floor.

From the launch on the north shore, near the dam, we paddled across the lake and explored the south shore as we headed east. We found two beaver lodges, and beaver paths and channels cut into the banks at regular intervals.

In July, thick beds of water shield cover the lake's east end. Paddling through this area is like paddling through thick green pea soup. Wood duck boxes dot the shore. At this time of year, water level determines how far you can paddle.

Beaver Meadows is a beautiful, isolated area surrounded by national forest. A thirty-seven-site campground is located near the lake. Half of the sites are open year-round. To reserve a site, call 1-800-283-CAMP. Primitive camping is permitted in many places in the national forest.

For more information, call the Allegheny National Forest District Office in Marienville at 814-927-6628.

NEARBY: While visiting Beaver Meadows, don't miss nearby Buzzard Swamp Wildlife Management Area. Located in the national forest and managed by the Game Commission, this area teems with water-fowl, waders, and shorebirds. The area features 8 miles of interconnecting trails through ponds, mudflats, food plots, and woodlots. To get there from Route 66 in Marienville, turn south on Loleta Road and drive 1.4 miles. Then turn left (east) onto Buzzard Swamp Road (at sign), and travel 2.5 miles on dirt road to the parking area.

Restaurant tip: Marienville is a small village with few eateries. We'd recommend Guisippe's Country Villa on Route 66 south of the Forest Service District Office and just north of the main intersection. We noticed a lot of Forest Service employees eating there, and we had excellent homemade food and dessert.

Another nearby area worth visiting is Cook Forest State Park south of Marienville on Route 36 in southern Forest County. This park features the Forest Cathedral, one of the state's largest stands of virgin timber (hemlock and white pine). We spent a wonderful night at Gateway Lodge, a privately owned country inn right inside the state park. For reservations, call 814-744-8017. If you're in the area, check out the Sawmill Center for the Arts and the Verna Leith Sawmill Theater, both in Cook Forest.

GETTING THERE: From Route 66 at Marienville, turn north onto Beaver Meadows Road. (There's a sign for the lake.) Drive 4.1 miles, then turn right at lake sign. **Or** we highly recommend the scenic approach to this lake through the Allegheny National Forest from Warren. Travel east on U.S. 6 for 13 miles. Turn west (right) on Route 666 in Sheffield and go 9.4 miles, then turn left at a stop sign, cross a bridge, and you are on Blue Jay Road. Proceed 1.2 miles, then make a hard right onto Job Corps Road. (From this point, you travel on dirt road all the way to the lake.) Go 5.4 miles, then turn left at the junction of five roads (toward Marienville). This junction is called Deadman Corner. Drive another 3.7 miles, then turn left at sign for Beaver Meadows. The launch is 1 mile in from the sign.

Between Deadman Corner and the lake access road, watch for a large area of dense shrubs and young growth. This was the site where several tornadoes touched down on May 31, 1985. The funnel clouds flattened 47 million board feet of timber, including 300-year-old hemlock and cherry trees. Much of the fallen timber was harvested and sold. About one mile past the tornado area, watch for a huge beaver dam and several large lodges on the left. These examples of animal engineering in a beautiful, swampy setting are simply awesome. Bring your camera!

As we took this scenic route, we stopped just past Deadman Corner to do some birding. An older gentleman in a pickup truck stopped to ask us if we were lost or needed help. It turned out that in 1936, as a member of the Civilian Conservation Corps, he had helped to build the Beaver Meadow Dam and also the Forest Service road we were traveling. In fact, he was on his way to a CCC reunion at Beaver Meadows.

North-Central Region

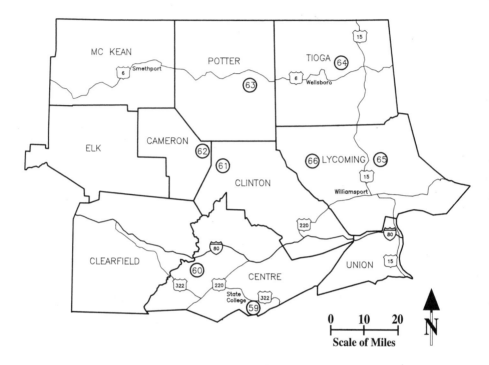

59. Colyer Lake

60. Black Moshannon Lake

61. Kettle Creek Reservoir

62. George B. Stevenson Reservoir

63. Lyman Lake

64. Hills Creek Lake

65. Rose Valley

66. Little Pine Lake

In a state of incredible beauty and diversity, the north-central region stands out in our minds as the area of superlatives. It's the most remote, most wooded, and most ruggedly beautiful part of Pennsylvania. Just getting there is a large part of the quiet water canoeing experience in this region. The drive through isolated mountain ranges provides a wonderful transition from the hectic pace of daily life to a quiet water retreat. We are always drawn, too, by the chance to explore the woods. State forest or state game lands surround most of the lakes in this region. Hiking trails, old logging roads, and abandoned railroad beds abound. Whenever we are canoeing in this area, we plan time for plenty of hiking on the Allegheny National Forest, on state game lands, and at state parks.

One of the region's most interesting towns is Williamsport, located along the Susquehanna River. Take time to view the Victorian homes along "Millionaire's Row." In the late nineteenth century, Williamsport was home to more millionaires than any other town in the country. Williamsport is also the birthplace of Little League Baseball and home of the Little League Museum.

Canoeists may wish to explore the 790-acre lake at Curwensville County Park in Clearfield County. This "lake" is actually a dammed portion of the Susquehanna River, West Branch. There is no limit on motorboat horsepower.

Colyer Lake

Size: 77 acres

RESTRICTIONS: nonpowered boats and electric motors only
MANAGING AGENCY: Fish and Boat Commission
LOCATION: near Tusseyville, Centre County

Tucked away in a mountainous setting, Colyer Lake, like many Fish Commission lakes, is a beautiful, isolated body of water that would be even prettier without the discarded Styrofoam bait containers and other litter left by careless fishermen. Maybe they'd place their litter in trash cans if the Fish Commission provided them. But it doesn't. And we have yet to see a public lake where people voluntarily and consistently carry out their own trash.

We're hopeful that public education will create a more concerned citizenry. Maybe if enough canoeists take a few minutes to pick up trash during each visit to a lake, we can put an end to this litter problem. We certainly left Colyer Lake cleaner than we found it.

Colyer is shaped like a three-fingered hand, with the palm of the hand at the north-end dam and the three fingers extending southward. The shoreline is almost completely wooded with pines and hardwoods.

Linda scans the lakeside vegetation for an elusive scarlet tanager at Colyer Lake.

In September and early October, the surrounding mountains flame with the fall colors.

We found several green-backed herons in the lake's middle finger. About the size of a crow, these common waterbirds prefer ponds, small lakes, wooded streams, and marshes with woodland cover. They often perch in trees along the water, so the canoeist who hugs the shorelines may be startled when one bursts from the trees with a loud "kyowk." We've noticed that green-backed herons tolerate us fairly well when we paddle gently and quietly and keep a little distance.

In addition to their green backs, the adults have a rich chestnut-colored neck and a white throat. The juveniles are heavily streaked around their chests and necks. We saw one adult and at least two juveniles at Colyer Lake, so we speculated that we had encountered a family group. One feature not easily seen is the bird's greenish black crest. But if you slowly float toward the bird, it will eventually become alarmed, start flicking its tail, and raise that dark crest before flying off. The herons at Colyer Lake were in a playful mood, it seemed, and they took turns flying to a perch shortly ahead of us, waiting until we had paddled close, then flying ahead to the next perch—hopscotch for herons.

GETTING THERE: Nine miles east of State College on U.S. 322, turn south at a low, inconspicuous lake sign onto Taylor Hill Road. Drive 1.3 miles to Lingle Road, turn right, and drive 0.5 mile to launch on north side, near dam.

Black Moshannon Lake
Size: 250 acres

RESTRICTIONS: nonpowered boats and electric motors only
MANAGING AGENCY: Black Moshannon State Park (3,394 acres)
LOCATION: near Phillipsburg, Centre County

The Black Moshannon is a lake within a bog within a state park within a state forest. It offers a fascinating glimpse of an unusual ecosystem. From its dam at the north, the narrow lake forks into two southern branches. Black Moshannon Bog Natural Area surrounds this southern portion, particularly the west fork.

The lake gets its name from the Indian name "Moss-hanne," meaning "moose stream." Its waters are "black" from tannin-producing sphagnum moss and oak leaves. This sphagnum moss is the dominant characteristic of a bog. Also characteristic are the leatherleaf and blueberry bushes, which line the shores of the southern forks. From a wooden boardwalk extending into the bog, visitors can also see sundew, bladderwort, pitcher plant, cut-grass, and sedges.

Beavers built the first dam creating Black Moshannon Lake. In the late nineteenth century, a lumber company constructed a dam on this original beaver dam site. Beavers are still very active on the lake and in the park. We saw two lodges in the southern portion, one along the west fork and one along the east fork. Several beaver dams can be seen along the creek that flows into the west fork. And beaver activity is reported in the bog natural area.

Bears frequent the area, too, although we did not see any. We did, however, find bear droppings among the low-bush blueberries blanketing Moss-Hanne Trail south of the lake.

Water lilies abound in the lake's southern waters. Both yellow and white species can be found side by side—the white lily pads floating on the water surface, the yellow lily pads emerging above. We discovered a beautiful pale pink variety of the white species. And several were bright pink. Just genetic variation at play here, according to Park Manager Chris Reese. We had never seen the pink flowers before and haven't seen any since.

We prefer the southernmost launch on the west shore. This launch is situated right where the lake forks. From here it's easy to explore both southern branches, each about a mile long.

Blooming water lilies brighten the shallows of most Pennsylvania lakes throughout the summer.

In summer, when the water level is low, it may not be possible to reach the end of the east fork. The water lilies grow thick here, as does the water shield plant. The water shield rests its football-shaped, two-inch-long leaves on the water, just like a white water lily. In fact, this plant is in the water lily family. Examine a plant and notice how the stem attaches to the middle (underside) of the leaf, not the end, like most plants. Note, too, the thick "mucous" film covering the plant's stem. This prevents the water shield from becoming waterlogged. The waxy coating on the top of the leaf accomplishes the same purpose and also helps prevent the leaf from drying out.

The west branch also supports great water lily beds. But canoeists can follow a water channel through the beds to the far end, where Black Moshannon Creek flows into the lake. It's a little like picking your way through a maze. But stay toward the east shore and you'll find the channel. Here the advantages of a canoe become very obvious. Depending on water level, it may even be possible to paddle into the adjoining creek. The beaver dams in this area could hinder your progress. But beaver dams are solid as rocks, so you can easily pull a canoe right up over one. And keep your eyes open for the rusty-colored swamp sparrow. We've seen several here.

Black Moshannon Lake ranks among our top five Pennsylvania lakes. This isolated wilderness area is a biological wonderland. Plan to camp here and spend several days. Canoe in the early morning or late evening to see the most wildlife. Walk the boardwalk and trails to explore the bog and surrounding woodlands. In the woods, watch for the huge, rotting tree stumps—victims of last century's lumber industry and reminders of a bygone age when giant hemlocks and white pine dominated Pennsylvania's north woods.

The state park features fourteen miles of interconnecting trails. And there are endless hiking opportunities in the surrounding Moshannon State Forest. Just remember to always carry a map along hiking trails. An eighty-site campground, rustic and modern cabins, a swimming beach, and a boat rental concession are also available.

For more information, call the park office at 814-342-5960 or the campground at 814-342-5967.

GETTING THERE: From I-80, take Exit 21 (Phillipsburg/Kylertown) and head north on Route 53 for about 0.5 mile. Turn right at park sign onto Munson Road, go 3.6 miles to a stop sign, turn left, then travel another 5.6 miles to the lake, at Route 504 bridge. Cross bridge and turn right to the park office (along lake's east shore) on Julian Pike. One launch site is about 0.5 mile past office. Two other launches are located along the west shore, off West Side Road on the other side of the bridge. **Or** from U.S. 322, west of State College, go north on U.S. 220 for 9.5 miles. (Ignore first park sign along the way.) Turn west on Route 504, then go 12.1 miles to lake. Turn left onto Julian Pike, just before bridge. This leads to park office and east-side launch.

Marshes and Muskrats

A marsh in winter is a quiet place. No colonies of red-winged blackbirds nesting in the cattails. No bullfrogs bellowing from the water's edge. No mosquitoes buzzing in your ear. No turtles basking in the sun, ready to drop loudly into the water when you venture too closely. No canoes splish-splashing through the channels. And if the water freezes, even ducks, geese, and herons abandon the marsh for open water farther south.

In midwinter a marsh seems a dead zone. And on the surface it is. But beneath the ice, fish swim (albeit less enthusiastically than they do in warmer weather) and muskrats go about their business of managing the marsh.

No animal is more important to a marsh than the muskrat. The collective appetite of the entire muskrat population determines how much of the marsh will remain open water and how much will be overgrown with cattails, bulrushes, and water lilies. Muskrats eat these and other aquatic plants.

When the muskrat population is low, aquatic plants prosper and take over the marsh. Open water disappears. When muskrat populations rebound and climb, they reduce the abundance of aquatic plants and create more open water. It's one of many natural life cycles. More muskrats eat more food. Soon there's not enough food to feed all the muskrats so they starve or move out, and the population declines. While the muskrat population bottoms out, aquatic vegetation rebounds. The increased food supply triggers population growth among the muskrats and their numbers increase. More muskrats eat more food. . . . And so it goes.

The consequences of all this extend far beyond muskrats and aquatic plants. Marshes act as natural sponges that absorb floodwaters, collect sediments, and filter pollutants from surface water and make it safe for human use. (That's why conservationists are always warning, "Save wetlands! Don't drain and develop them!")

Kettle Creek Reservoir
Size: 160 acres

RESTRICTIONS: nonpowered and electric motors only
MANAGING AGENCY: Kettle Creek State Park (1,793 acres)
LOCATION: Clinton County

The scenic wilderness drive through wild and rugged Sproul State Forest would be reason enough to visit Kettle Creek Reservoir. But the reservoir itself is worth the trip. Tucked in the mountains, Kettle Creek Reservoir forms an L, extending west and then northeast from its dam. Its total length is about 2 miles, with 4.5 miles of shoreline. Along the lake's steeply wooded east shore, the pine, hemlock, and oak forest meets the water's edge, except for a large meadow near the dam. Kettle Creek Road parallels the western shoreline, with a narrow wooded strip separating the road and the water. The reservoir is noted for good water quality and excellent trout and bass fishing.

The launch is at the north end, where Kettle Creek enters the reservoir. From here you can head south to explore the reservoir or paddle north into an extensive marshy area at the creek's headwaters. We saw

Kettle Creek Reservoir winds long and narrow through the mountains in the wild and rugged 278,000-acre Sproul State Forest.

several fishermen in rowboats at various points along the reservoir, but as usual, we had the marsh to ourselves. Except for the green-backed and great blue herons.

We paddled into Kettle Creek and headed upstream for almost two miles, getting out several times to drag the canoe over shallow areas. These miniportages usually aren't necessary in the spring and early summer. Kettle Creek enjoys a reputation as an excellent trout stream—one of many surrounding the park. If you decide to follow the creek upstream, take a park map. The creek divides into several different channels along the way.

Kettle Creek Lake lies 3.5 miles south of the reservoir. This beautiful, wooded seven-acre lake features a lovely lakeside campground. The fishing here is reportedly good, and we saw several families whose young children fished the lake and rode their bikes along sleepy campground roads. It looked like the perfect place to pitch a tent for a week or two. You can even canoe this lake, although seven acres isn't a lot of room to maneuver around in. The 53-mile Donut Hole Hiking Trail passes right through the campground as it meanders its way through Sproul State Forest. The forty-site campground features ten electrical hookups and a trailer dump station and is open from early April through December.

Another campground is located on the western shore of the reservoir. This one, open from trout season in April until mid-October, contains forty sites, with pit toilets and water hydrants.

Many miles of hiking trails can be found in the park and surrounding 278,000-acre Sproul State Forest. Watch for bears, bobcats, porcupines, and osprey. Kettle Creek Kanoe Rentals rents canoes for either lake or whitewater trips (717-923-0780).

For more information, call the park office at 717-923-0206.

NEARBY: At the dam overlook, observe how the Army Corps of Engineers sliced through the mountain to construct the roadway and dam. The resulting cliffs support phoebe and swallow nests.

For a scenic overlook of the reservoir, drive 3.5 miles west on Sugar Camp Road, near the amphitheater.

Scenic Kettle Creek, the reservoir's feeder stream, is an excellent trout stream between Kettle Creek Lake and Kettle Creek Reservoir and again north of the reservoir. But acid mine drainage seriously affects the creek's fish life south of the lower campground.

GETTING THERE: From U.S. 220 at Lock Haven, take Route 120 West, which is the scenic Bucktail Trail. (This trail, now a road, is actually a state park.) Go 36.5 miles, then turn right at park sign in Westport onto Kettle Creek Road. Drive 6.2 miles to park entrance. Here, a campground and seasonal nature center are located along a seven-acre lake. Continue another 3.5 miles north to the reservoir, another campground, and boat launch.

CAUTION: The low-lying road along the reservoir is subject to flash flooding. If you are visiting in the spring or after heavy rains, call before you drive in. There is a major flood here every few years, according to park office employees.

George B. Stevenson Reservoir

Size: 140 acres

RESTRICTIONS: nonpowered boats and electric motors only
MANAGING AGENCY: Sinnemahoning State Park (1,910 acres)
LOCATION: near Sinnemahoning, Cameron County

When we pulled into the parking lot at the boat launch on Sinnemahoning State Park's George B. Stevenson Reservoir and saw a mature bald eagle perched across the narrow lake, we knew we'd hit a winner. This reservoir teems with wildlife. Several members of a small group of "eagle watchers" told us that the lake has become a regular feeding ground for bald eagles.

After watching the adult perched in a snag for several minutes, we discovered another individual in a nearby tree when it swooped from its pine perch toward the water. The absence of a white head and tail identified it as a juvenile. It appeared to be fishing but failed to catch anything. Perhaps it was still learning. It glided along the shoreline, then swept up onto its perch.

Stevenson Dam was built in the 1950s to control flooding in the Susquehanna River basin. The resulting reservoir extends about 1.5 miles northwest from this dam on the First Fork Sinnemahoning Creek. Sinnemahoning is a Native American word meaning "rocky lick"—an area where animals apparently found salt. Elk State Forest surrounds the reservoir and state forest, and from the water, canoeists can enjoy incredible vistas of mountain peaks.

The launch site is toward the north end of the lake. After heading south to explore the reservoir's wooded shoreline and a small cove along the east shore, we paddled north of the launch. Two long, narrow, grassy islands divide the reservoir's northern end into three channels. As we slipped through the middle one we noticed that the island's muddy banks were riddled with large holes. Could be beavers, we concluded. We flushed a green-backed heron. And kingfishers chattered and fished all along the way.

Suddenly the water ahead rippled, and we focused our binoculars. A river otter! We watched it dive and surface three times, then climb upon the easternmost island and slip into the grass. Nearby we found a mud slide of the kind otters love to make. Later we discovered that otters had indeed been released in area streams. It thrilled us to learn

Bald eagles, river otters, porcupines, and belted kingfishers are just a few of the animals we saw during our visit to George B. Stevenson Reservoir in Sinnemahoning State Park.

that they were surviving. Local people, however, often dislike otters because they say otters eat game fish.

Unfortunately, river otters often get a bad rap from fishermen. Though these overgrown members of the weasel family are indeed primarily piscivorous, crayfish, frogs, waterfowl, and many other aquatic animals are also important foods. Furthermore, food habit studies of otters consistently report three interesting trends: (1) Otters do not specialize in particular species of fish; (2) they typically eat the species that are most abundant in any given area; and (3) they eat slow-swimming fish more often than faster-swimming fish. In other words, otters eat whatever happens to be easiest to catch. Consequently, they eat many more suckers, carp, shiners, sunfish, and catfish than they do trout, bass, or pike.

In spring and early summer, it's possible to follow Sinnemahoning Creek upstream for quite a distance. The current is swift and paddling can be rough, but the view is spectacular. In midsummer we made it several hundred yards upstream. Here we found more kingfishers, a nesting colony of cedar waxwings, several big largemouth bass (the water is crystal clear), spotted sandpipers working the gravelly stream

sides, a Louisiana waterthrush bobbing along water's edge, a Cooper's hawk soaring overhead, and the washed-out remains of a beaver lodge.

Heading south again, the view becomes even grander. The steep mountain peaks to the south give the feeling of a castle or fortress. The shorelines are steeply wooded all the way to the dam. A deer browsed quietly in a cove as we glided past.

Later, as we were leaving the park, a young otter crossed the road ahead of us. And several miles farther down the road, we saw a mink, smaller and darker than the otter, just avoid an oncoming car. We also saw two dead porcupines on the road.

Sinnemahoning State Park features a thirty-five-site campground, a swimming beach, picnic areas, and hiking trails. But be careful; timber rattlesnakes and black bears inhabit the area.

For more information, call the park office at 814-647-8401.

NEARBY: The remains of the old Austin Dam is located north of the park along Route 872. Austin Dam broke in 1911, killing eighty-nine people and destroying much of Austin.

South of the park is Bucktail State Park, a scenic seventy-five-mile drive along Route 120 between Emporium and Lock Haven.

GETTING THERE: From U.S. 220 at Lock Haven, take Route 120 West (the scenic Bucktail Trail) for 54.9 miles to Route 872. Turn right (there's a park sign) and drive 7.5 miles to park entrance and overlook. Drive another mile to the Eagle Watch area, park office, and boat launch. **Or** from U.S. 6 east of Coudersport, head south for 33 miles on Route 872 to park office and launch.

Lyman Lake

Size: 45 acres

RESTRICTIONS: nonpowered boats and electric motors only
MANAGING AGENCY: Lyman Run State Park (595 acres)
LOCATION: near Galeton, Potter County

Its shorelines are regular and its surface area is small, but Lyman Lake is a perfect spot to combine family canoeing and camping. Located in some of the most remote forest land Pennsylvania has to offer, Lyman Lake supports an interesting diversity of wildlife, including four species of trout. The lake extends west from its dam and ends in a series of small coves at the headwaters of Lyman Run. Here we saw kingfishers diving for their supper and an inordinate number of painted turtles basking in the late afternoon sun. There were turtles on almost every log, rock, and tree stump emerging from the water. A soft "plip, plip" accompanied our paddles as the turtles slipped into the water at our approach. A beaver lodge perched prominently on the south shore.

The lake's southern shoreline is wooded, while Lyman Run Road hugs the north shore. An early Civilian Conservation Corp (CCC) camp was located along Lyman Run in the area of the park. The park features two campgrounds with drinking water and comfort stations. There is also a swimming beach, a boat rental concession, and hiking trails. Susquehannock State Forest surrounds the park, and there are miles of remote state forest roads to explore.

We enjoyed Rock Run Road, an unpaved forest road that runs north from the park to U.S. 6. The road climbs a mountain just outside of the park and offers a wonderful vista of the lake below.

NEARBY: We highly recommend a visit to the Pennsylvania Lumber Museum, just twelve miles from Lyman Run State Park, along U.S. 6. This museum contains a reconstruction of an early logging camp, and you can tour it at your own pace with an interpretive brochure. Children especially enjoy the chance to walk through the different buildings and see and touch many artifacts from bygone days. Inside the main building are photographs and interpretive displays. Another fascinating feature is the extensive exhibit depicting life in a CCC camp. The CCC built many of the dams on the lakes we canoe and constructed many of the state park facilities, roads, and hiking trails we enjoy, so it was fun to learn more about the corps.

Also nearby is Ole Bull State Park along Kettle Creek in the "Black Forest" of Potter County. The hiking and fly-fishing here are superb.

GETTING THERE: Take U.S. 6 east for 5.2 miles from its intersection with Route 872, near Coudersport. Turn right on Lyman Run Road and drive eight miles on dirt road to launch at the eastern end of lake near the dam. *Or* from Coudersport, travel east on U.S. 6 14.8 miles, turn south (right), and immediately right again onto Rock Run Road (a state forest road that is unmarked at this intersection). Drive 7.6 miles to park and launch.

Hills Creek Lake

Size: 137 acres

RESTRICTIONS: nonpowered and electric motors only
MANAGING AGENCY: Hills Creek State Park (406 acres)
LOCATION: near Mansfield, Tioga County

When we think of Hills Creek Lake, we think of beavers. It's one of the easiest places in the state to see these large rodents—if you stick around until dusk. Even before we reached the lake we saw a huge beaver lodge on Hills Creek, just south of the park.

With its dam at the south end, the lake extends north and ends in a series of marshy coves blanketed with water lilies. The beavers seem to prefer these northern coves; we found two active lodges here. The vegetation and sediment in this beaver marsh is reportedly twenty feet deep in some places.

The west shoreline is fairly straight, while large coves create an irregular east shoreline. The lake's southeast corner is marshy, supporting bur reed and viburnums, white spruce, red osier dogwood, and other moisture-loving species. Toward the south end, a peninsula cuts the lake almost in half. This is where the swimming beach, boat rental concession, picnic area, and campground are located.

Dusk is the best time to view beavers, so we launched from the northernmost access early one evening. Apparently the word is out on the beavers. As the sun set behind the wooded shoreline, a crowd of campers appeared and parked themselves on the bank behind the lodge. But we had the best seats on the lake.

As we floated on the darkening lake, four different beavers munched lily pads and pondweed nearby. When our canoe drifted too close to one, it slapped its tail and dove under the canoe. It resurfaced not twenty feet from us and slapped and dove again. And a third time. What a show! And even with all the commotion around our canoe, three other beavers close to us continued to eat their lily pad dinner. We could actually hear the crunching sound.

A full moon rose over the lake that night, and we sat among the lily pads, transfixed. Night sounds filled the air—the "banjo-plucking" green frogs, the bullfrogs' deep "jug-o'-rum," the beavers' steady crunching of lily pads. Then, overhead, we heard the soft whistling of wings as a small flight of ducks passed in the moon glow. Finally,

Sunset at Hills Creek Lake brings out flashing fireflies, tail-slapping beavers, and hooting owls.

reluctantly, we added our own sounds—the dip and drip of our paddles as we headed for shore.

The lake, originally part of an area known as Kelly's Swamp, supports an excellent warm-water fishery, and fishing is popular here.

For more information, call the park office at 717-724-4246.

GETTING THERE: From U.S. 6, about 3 miles east of Wellsboro, turn north onto S.R. 4035 at park sign. Go 1.1 miles, turn right at T onto S.R. 4002. Go 0.4 mile, bear left onto S.R. 4037 at park sign, and drive 2.6 miles. Bear left at park sign and drive another 0.5 mile to the park entrance at the dam. Continue driving, past the entrance, to launches on the lake's west side. There is a separate launch for campers on the east side.

Beavers

The amber sun set beyond the ridge and dusk quickly enveloped the valley. As I packed the tackle box, Linda noticed a dark form lumbering down the bank on the edge of the lake. But when it slid, almost silently, into one of the stream's deeper pools, I recognized North America's largest rodent—a beaver.

It swam quietly past the canoe, just twenty feet away, and seemed to ignore us. But just as we noted its apparent disinterest, it sounded an alarm announcing an unwelcome intruder—"Slap!"

The beaver smacked its broad, flat tail on the surface of the water, then dove under for cover. If any other beavers were nearby, they heard the warning. Several minutes later the beaver surfaced again, slapped another alarm, and submerged. We took the hint, finished packing our gear, and headed for the car. No fresh fish for dinner, but the beaver tale made great conversation.

Beavers are adapted to spend most of their time underwater. Large webbed hind feet make them graceful swimmers. They use movable double claws on the two inside toes of each hind foot as combs to groom their thick luxurious fur. Special valves close their nostrils and ears when they dive underwater. Nictitating membranes, clear inner eyelids that protect their eyes while swimming, enable them to see while submerged. And their lips close behind their large incisors so they can eat underwater. This is particularly important during the winter, when they store their entire food supply under the frozen lake near the lodge.

The natural history of beavers is legendary. Nature's engineers, beavers build sophisticated dams, lodges, and canals. They manipulate their environment for their own benefit more than any other animal, save man.

The story begins when a pair of beavers find a nice grove of aspens, alders, or willows along a stream. Using their huge incisors like a chain saw, they cut trees and float logs and branches into position to build the foundation of a dam. As the patchwork of sticks grows, the beavers reinforce it with mud and rocks, until it's capable of holding back water. In time, a pond forms behind the dam.

The rising water level behind the dam stimulates beavers to build a large fortress-like lodge. The only entrance to the lodge is underwater, so it provides safe haven from predators—such as bobcats, coyotes, and great-horned owls—and warmth even through the coldest winter storms. It also makes a snug nursery for the three or four walnut-sized kits that are born in May or June to attentive, monogamous parents.

The pond's deeper water serves several other purposes. It provides cold storage for a supply of food that lasts the winter. Beavers clip and store fresh aquatic vegetation and succulent branches of their favorite trees underwater near the entrance to the lodge. During the winter, when the surface of the pond is frozen, they slip into the icy waters and subsist on their underwater cache.

The beavers' engineering skill changes the vegetation within hundreds of yards of the dam. The changing vegetation alters the animal communities as well. As the pond grows, the area's soil chemistry is altered, and water-tolerant trees such as willows, birch, aspen, and alders invade. Not surprisingly, all are favorite beaver foods. The pond itself attracts wood ducks, black ducks, muskrats, mink, trout, and other fish. An avid fly fisherman who knows a secluded beaver pond guards that information dearly.

Eventually, though, beavers deplete the food supply in the immediate area around the pond and they move on. Over time, the dam may deteriorate and break, allowing the pond to revert to a meandering stream. Or the pond may fill in. This can take decades. Siltation continues until the pond disappears and new ground is born. In about 150 years the original forest, complete with its cast of plant and animals characters, returns. In the blink of an ecological eye, nature cycles.

Some beavers forgo a lodge and live in burrows they excavate along a stream bank or lake shoreline. In the absence of dams and lodges, beavers' presence often goes undetected. Others build their lodge on the edge of large lakes. You will see many of these lakeside lodges on the lakes described in this book.

The beaver's greatest impacts on man have been historical, social, and economic. The first explorers to penetrate the western edges of North America did so in search of beaver pelts, which were in great demand in Europe. (Recall Pasquinel from Michener's *Centennial.*) The utility, beauty, and warmth of beaver skins influenced European and American fashion. The fur trade drove the economies of the towns and trading posts on the western fringes of an emerging nation. Fortunes were made and empires built on the fur of the beaver.

By 1900, beavers had been exterminated over most of their range. Thanks to sound wildlife management, however, beavers have come back strong. In some areas today, their dams and the flooding they cause make them unwelcome pests. See for yourself just how well beavers are doing when you paddle almost any Pennsylvania lake in the glow of the setting sun.

Rose Valley Lake
Size: 396 acres

RESTRICTIONS: nonpowered boats and electric motors only
MANAGING AGENCY: Fish and Boat Commission
LOCATION: near Trout Run, Lycoming County

As we drove up the steep windy mountain road en route to Rose Valley Lake, we realized we were climbing to a high mountain valley. Nestled between the mountains, Rose Valley Lake is the prize at the end of a drive through spectacular countryside. The lake reminds us of a giant arrowhead pointing north. The arrowhead has serrated edges, which are large coves along the east and west shorelines.

Much of the western shoreline meets rolling farm fields against a backdrop of mountain peaks. Marshy vegetation covers the lake's wide southern end, and its narrow northern tip becomes marshy, too. Lake Road crosses the northern tip, and you can paddle under the bridge into an area of bur reed, cattails, and emergent stumps.

Rose Valley Lake stretches at least one-half mile wide at its widest point. This is a large body of water. And like any large body of water, this one is sensitive to the least bit of wind. Perhaps that's why it's so popular with the weekend sailboat set. Windblown whitecaps that mean smooth sailing for some, however, can seriously challenge canoeists. We struggled to stay on course the afternoon we paddled this lake, and there was only a gentle breeze. Usually we hug the shoreline on open lakes like this one, but that day we wanted to get from Point A (the southern launch) to Point B (the marshy northern tip) in the shortest time possible, so we decided to paddle a straight line through open waters. As we paddled north through the deep, choppy water, we were both glad to be wearing our personal flotation devices (PFDs). Wearing PFDs is such a habit that we usually don't even think about it, except in situations where we feel a little vulnerable. We can't stress enough how important it is for canoeists to wear PFDs. And don't even *think* about putting a child into a canoe without a PFD.

We really liked this beautiful lake but fear it may soon be overrun by vacationers because it is so close to Williamsport. Also, large, beautiful homes seem to be cropping up all over the nearby farmlands. We'd suggest a weekday visit to Rose Valley.

GETTING THERE: From U.S. 15, north of Williamsport, take exit for Trout Run. Head north on Route 14 for 0.25 mile, turn right (east) on Trout Run Road (S.R. 1002). Drive 2.5 miles up a steep windy mountain and turn left at T onto S.R. 1001. Go 0.6 mile, then turn right onto Trimble Road. Go 1.9 miles to main access and first launch at south end of lake. Two more launches, one on the east shore and one at the northwest corner, can both be reached by continuing around the lake on Lake Road.

Little Pine Lake

Size: 94 acres

RESTRICTIONS: nonpowered and electric motors only
MANAGING AGENCY: Little Pine State Park (2,158 acres)
LOCATION: near Waterville, Lycoming County

Just when we thought we'd seen the most spectacular lakes Pennsylvania has to offer, along comes Little Pine Lake in the heart of the Appalachian Mountains region. Historically, environmentally, aesthetically, and recreationally, Little Pine Lake is a fantastic place.

The lake is fed by Little Pine Creek, an offshoot of *the* Pine Creek that flows through the Pennsylvania Grand Canyon farther north. During the late-nineteenth and early twentieth centuries, loggers used the Little Pine to float logs to Williamsport sawmills.

Like so many other creeks and streams in this region, Little Pine Creek was dammed in response to the 1936 flood that devastated Williamsport, Jersey Shore, and surrounding communities. But natural disasters continued to plague this area. Hurricane Agnes destroyed much of the CCC-built state park facilities in June 1972. And in 1989, gale-force winds flattened hundreds of trees in the campground south of the dam.

From its south-end dam, Little Pine Lake stretches long and narrow through a steep mountain valley for nearly two miles. Mixed hardwood and coniferous forest covers the eastern and most of the western shores. You'll see oak, white and red pine, hemlock, maple, hickory, white and paper birch, sycamore, and poplar. Marshland characterizes the lake's north end, and we explored a series of channels cutting through the vegetation. Then we worked our way west to the main channel of Little Pine Creek, where it enters the lake.

The Little Pine is very canoeable in the spring and early summer. You can follow the creek for miles through the valley when the water is up. It's home to native and stocked trout and other game fish. S.R. 4001 parallels the creek all the way to the village of English Center.

A small swimming beach, a boat concession, and a picnic area are located on the lake's east shore. A 105-site campground is located just south of the dam. And there are miles of hiking trails through the park—some quite rugged and steep, all scenic. Many of the trails hook up with trails through the Tiadaghton State Forest, which surrounds the park. It's a rugged, breathtakingly beautiful area. Our only regret was that we hadn't planned a longer stay.

NEARBY: Algerine Swamp Natural Area, a glacial bog containing black spruce, balsam fir, and other northern species, straddles Lycoming and Tioga counties in Tiadaghton State Forest. This eighty-four-acre area is well worth the trip. It's located northwest along Gamble Run Road, off Route 414, which follows Pine Creek. Large portions of Route 414 are dirt, and the road is literally carved out of the mountainside in some spots. This is a remote, wild portion of Pennsylvania and truly one of the most magnificent parts of the state we've ever seen.

Also nearby is the Grand Canyon of Pennsylvania, which can be seen from Colton Point or Leonard Harrison State Parks. The Grand Canyon, also known as Pine Creek Gorge, was formed thousands of years ago when melting glaciers cut through the area. Steep, rocky cliffs rise about 1,000 feet above Pine Creek, which winds its way through the narrow gorge. There's only room for the creek and the railroad tracks that run alongside.

Little Pine Lake winds through some of Pennsylvania's most remote and spectacular mountain wilderness.

Hyner View State Park to the west (Clinton County) is the site of an annual Flaming Foliage Festival and hang gliding competitions.

For more information, call the state park office at 717-753-8209.

GETTING THERE: From Rt. 15 at Buttonwood exit, head west on Route 284 for 9.5 miles. Bear to the left onto Route 287 South for 1.1 miles. Turn right at park sign onto S.R. 4001, then travel 0.5 mile. Turn left at bridge, and continue on S.R. 4001 for 7.6 miles to the launch.

Appendix A
Pennsylvania Quiet Water Review At A Glance

NORTHEAST REGION

Lake	Size (acres)	County	Managing Agency
Bradys Lake	229	Monroe	Fish and Boat Commission
Tobyhanna Lake	170	Monroe	Tobyhanna State Park
Gouldsboro Lake	250	Monroe	Gouldsboro State Park
Mauch Chunk Lake	345	Carbon	Mauch Chunk Lake Park/ Fish and Boat Commission
Lake Jean	245	Luzerne	Rickett's Glen State Park
Hunters Lake	117	Sullivan	Fish and Boat Commission
Stevens Lake	62	Wyoming	Fish and Boat Commission
Stephen Foster Lake	75	Bradford	Mt Pisgah State Park
Lakawanna Lake	210	Lakawanna	Lakawanna State Park
Belmont Lake	172	Wayne	Fish and Boat Commission
Miller Pond	61	Wayne	Fish and Boat Commission
Upper Woods Pond	90	Wayne	Fish and Boat Commission
White Oak Pond	175	Wayne	Fish and Boat Commission
Shohola Lake	1,100	Pike	Game Commission
Pecks Pond	315	Pike	Bureau of Forestry
Promised Land Lake	422	Pike	Promised Land State Park

SOUTHEAST REGION

Lake	Size (acres)	County	Managing Agency
Lake Nockamixon	1,450	Bucks	Nockamixon State Park
Green Lane Reservoir	805	Montgomery	Green Lane Reservoir Park
Hopewell Lake	68	Berks	French Creek State Park
Scotts Run Lake	21	Berks	French Creek State Park

SOUTHEAST REGION (cont.)

Lake	Size (acres)	County	Managing Agency
Marsh Creek Lake	535	Chester	Marsh Creek State Park
Speedwell Forge Lake	106	Lancaster	Fish and Boat Commission
Lake Redman	290	York	William H. Kane Park
Lake Williams	220	York	William H. Kane Park
Lake Marburg	1,275	York	Codorus State Park
L.B. Sheppard Reservoir	240	York	Fish and Boat Commission
Pinchot Lake	340	York	Gifford Pinchot State Park
Tuscarora Lake	96	Schuylkill	Tuscorora State Park
Leaser Lake	117	Lehigh	Fish and Boat Commission

SOUTH-CENTRAL REGION

Lake	Size (acres)	County	Managing Agency
Letterkenny Reservoir	54	Franklin	Fish and Boat Commission
Cowans Gap Lake	42	Fulton	Cowans Gap State Park
Meadow Grounds Lake	204	Fulton	Fish and Boat Commission
Shawnee Lake	451	Bedford	Shawnee State Park
Canoe Lake	155	Blair	Canoe Creek State Park
Stone Valley Lake	72	Huntingdon	Penn State University
Walker Lake	239	Snyder	Fish and Boat Commission
Opossum Lake	59	Cumberland	Fish and BoatCommission
Laurel Lake	25	Cumberland	Pine Grove Furnace State Park

SOUTHWEST REGION

Lake	Size (acres)	County	Managing Agency
Lake Somerset	253	Somerset	Fish and Boat Commission
Cranberry Glade Lake	112	Somerset	Fish and Boat Commission
R.J. Duke Lake	62	Greene	Ryerson Station State Park
Dutch Fork Lake	91	Washington	Fish and Boat Commission

SOUTHWEST REGION (cont.)

Lake	Size (acres)	County	Managing Agency
Cross Creek Lake	258	Washington	Cross Creek Cty. Park/ Fish and Boat Commission
Raccoon Lake	101	Beaver	Raccoon Creek State Park
Yellow Creek Lake	720	Indiana	Yellow Creek State Park
Glendale Lake	1,600	Cambria	Prince Gallitzin State Park

NORTHWEST REGION

Lake	Size (acres)	County	Managing Agency
Lake Arthur	3,225	Butler	Moraine State Park
Glade Wildlife Lake	400	Butler	Game Commission
Kahle Lake	250	Venango	Fish and Boat Commission
Lake Wilhelm	1,860	Mercer	Maurice K. Goddard State Park
Conneaut Marsh	5,619	Crawford	Game Commission
Pymatuning Reservoir	16,500	Crawford	Pymatuning State Park
Tamarack Lake	562	Crawford	Fish and Boat Commission
Pool 9	130	Crawford	Erie National Wildlife Refuge
Woodcock Creek Lake	500	Crawford	Army Corps of Engineers
Presque Isle Lagoons		Erie	Presque Isle State Park
Lake Pleasant	60	Erie	Private/Fish and Boat Commission access
Union City Reservoir	60	Erie	Union City
Chapman Lake	68	Warren	Chapman State Park
Beaver Meadows Lake	50	Forest	Allegheny National Forest

NORTH-CENTRAL REGION

Lake	Size (acres)	County	Managing Agency
Colyer Lake	77	Centre	Fish Commission
Black Moshannon Lake	250	Centre	Black Moshannon State Park
Kettle Creek Reservoir	160	Clinton	Kettle Creek State Park

NORTH-CENTRAL REGION (cont.)

Lake	Size (acres)	County	Managing Agency
George B. Stevenson Reservoir	140	Cameron	Sinnemahoning State Park
Lyman Lake	45	Potter	Lyman Run State Park
Hills Creek Lake	137	Tioga	Hills Creek State Park
Rose Valley Lake	396	Lycoming	Fish Commission
Little Pine Lake	94	Lycoming	Little Pine State Park

Appendix B
For More Information

For those who might like more information about Pennsylvania's quiet water and its natural history, here's a short list of useful references.

Allen, W.B., Jr. "The Snakes of Pennsylvania." *Reptile & Amphibian Magazine*, 1992.

Brauning, D.W., ed. *Atlas of Breeding Birds in Pennsylvania.* Pittsburgh: University of Pittsburgh Press, 1992.

Klots, E.B. *The New Field Book of Freshwater Life.* New York: G.P. Putnam's Sons, 1966.

Merritt, J.F. *Guide to the Mammals of Pennsylvania.* Pittsburgh: University of Pittsburgh Press, 1987.

Niering, W.A. *The Audubon Society Nature Guides: Wetlands.* New York: Alfred A. Knopf, 1985.

Pennsylvania Atlas and Gazetteer. Freeport, ME: DeLorme Mapping Co., 1990.

Pennsylvania Fish and Boat Commission. *Guide to Public Fishing Waters and Boating Access*. Harrisburg, PA: Pennsylvania Fish and Boat Commission, 1993.

Shaffer, L.L. *Pennsylvania Amphibians and Reptiles.* Pennsylvania Fish Commission. 1991.

Shalaway, S.D. *Birds, Bats, Butterflies . . . and Other Backyard Beasts.* Cameron, WV: Saddle Ridge Press, 1992.

Thompson, P. *Thompson's Guide to Freshwater Fishes.* Boston: Houghton Mifflin Co., 1985.

The Peterson Field Guide series published by the Houghton Mifflin Co.

The Peterson First Guide series published by the Houghton Mifflin Co.

Golden Guide series published by Golden Press.

About the Authors

SCOTT SHALAWAY holds a Ph.D. in wildlife ecology from Michigan State University and has taught at both Oklahoma State University and the University of Oklahoma. He now makes his living as a freelance writer. His syndicated nature column now reaches more than one million readers each week in more than twenty newspapers, and he writes regularly for several national and regional magazines. He also hosts a weekly radio talk show called *The Wild Side*. This is his third book.

LINDA SHALAWAY earned a B.A. in English and Journalism at the University of Delaware and is now a high school English teacher and freelance writer and editor. She specializes in educational and natural history topics. This is her second book.

The Shalaways grew up in rural Montgomery County, Pennsylvania and now live on a ridge near Cameron, West Virginia. They have two daughters, Nora and Emma.

About the AMC

The Appalachian Mountain Club pursues a vigorous conservation agenda while encouraging responsible recreation, based on the philosophy that succcessful, long-term conservation depends upon firsthand experience of the natural environment. Sixty thousand members have joined the AMC to pursue their interests in hiking, canoeing, skiing, walking, rock climbing, bicycling, camping, kayaking, and backpacking, and—at the same time—to help safeguard the environment in which these activities are possible.

Since it was founded in 1876, the Club has been at the forefront of the environmental protection movement. By cofounding several of New England's leading environmental organizations, and working in coalition with these and many more groups, the AMC has positively influenced legislation and public opinion.

Volunteers in each chapter lead hundreds of outdoor activities and excursions and offer introductory instruction in backcountry sports. The AMC education department offers members and the public a wide range of workshops, from introductory camping to the intensive Mountain Leadership School taught on the trails of the White Mountains.

The most recent efforts in the AMC conservation program include river protection, Northern Forest Lands policy, Sterling Forest (NY) preservation, and support for the Clean Air Act.

The AMC's research department focuses on the forces affecting the ecosystem, including ozone levels, acid rain and fog, climate change, rare flora and habitat protection, and air quality and visibility.

AMC Trails

The AMC trails program maintains over 1,400 miles of trail (including 350 miles of the Appalachian Trail) and more than 50 shelters in the Northeast. Through a coordinated effort of volunteers, seasonal crews, and program staff, the AMC contributes more than 10,000 hours of public service work each summer in the area from Washington, D.C. to Maine.

In addition to supporting our work by becoming an AMC member, hikers can donate time as volunteers. The club offers four unique weekly volunteer base camps in New Hampshire, Maine, Massachusetts, and New York. We also sponsor ten-day service projects throughout the United States, Adopt-a-Trail programs, trails day events, trail skills workshops, and chapter and camp volunteer projects.

The AMC has a longstanding connection to Acadia National Park. Working in cooperation with the National Park Service and Friends of Acadia, the AMC Trails Program provides many opportunities to preserve the park's resources. These include half-day volunteer projects for guests at AMC's Echo Lake Camp, ten-day service projects, week-long volunteer crews in the fall, and trails day events. For more information on these public service volunteer opportunities, contact the AMC Trails Program, Pinkham Notch Visitor Center, P.O. Box 298, Gorham NH 03581; 603-466-2721.

The club operates eight alpine huts in the White Mountains that provide shelter, bunks and blankets, and hearty meals for hikers. Pinkham Notch Visitor Center, at the foot of Mt. Washington, is base camp to the adventurous and the ideal location for individuals and families new to outdoor recreation. Comfortable bunkrooms, mountain hospitality, and home-cooked, family-style meals make Pinkham Notch Visitor Center a fun and affordable choice for lodging. For reservations, call 603-466-2727.

At the AMC headquarters in Boston and at Pinkham Notch Visitor Center in New Hampshire, the bookstore and information center stock the entire line of AMC publications, as well as other trail and river guides, maps, reference materials, and the latest articles on conservation issues. Guidebooks and other AMC gifts are available by mail order (AMC, P.O. Box 298, Gorham NH 03581), or call toll-free 800-262-4455. Also available from the bookstore or by subscription is *Appalachia,* the country's oldest mountaineering and conservation journal.

Alphabetical Listing of Lakes and Ponds